Economic Rationality

What is Political Economy? series

Economic Rationality

Stephen Engelmann

polity

First published in 2022 by Polity Press

Polity Press
65 Bridge Street
Cambridge CB2 1UR, UK

Polity Press
111 River Street
Hoboken, NJ 07030, USA

ISBN-13: 978-1-5095-3810-2 (hardback)
ISBN-13: 978-1-5095-3811-9 (paperback)

A catalogue record for this book is available from the British Library.

Library of Congress Control Number: 2022935234

Typeset in 10.5 on 12 pt Sabon
by Fakenham Prepress Solutions, Fakenham, Norfolk NR21 8NL
Printed and bound in Great Britain by CPI Group (UK) Ltd, Croydon

For further information on Polity, visit our website:
politybooks.com

Contents

To Mia, with love and hope

Acknowledgments

I have enjoyed a huge amount of support for this book from the beginning. A National Endowment for the Humanities University Faculty Fellowship launched the interdisciplinary journey that led to it. George Owers, formerly of Polity, solicited the proposal and saw much of the project through. The Press has been tremendous: in addition to Owers I thank Laura Booth, Susan Beer, Julia Davies, Evie Deavall, and their colleagues, as well as anonymous reviewers at proposal and manuscript stages. Research and writing for *Economic Rationality* were made possible by a residential fellowship at the University of Illinois at Chicago's Institute for the Humanities in 2019–2020, with additional support from UIC's College of Liberal Arts and Sciences, the Department of Political Science, a Chancellor's Undergraduate Research Award, and an Award for Creative Activity. Many works old and new not named in the notes were helpful to my research, including resources through the Institute for New Economic Thinking's History of Economic Thought website, the Liberty Fund's Online Library of Liberty, and the University of Illinois at Chicago's Daley Library and its I-Share partners. For the opportunity to present pieces of the project as it developed I thank: Michael Quinn, Philip Schofield, and the audience at University College London; Alba Alexander, colleagues, and students from UIC's Department of Political Science; Mark Canuel, Laura Hostetler, Linda Vavra, and audiences from UIC's Institute for the Humanities; Nils Goldschmidt, Mark McAdam, Deirdre McCloskey, and colleagues from the

Sunday Seminar; panelists and audience at the 2022 Western Political Science Association meetings; and Malte Dold, students, and colleagues at Pomona College. Students in my political economy seminars have been an inspiration, and from early on many individuals helped in big and small ways; some are strong-minded but tolerant and generous economists, and they especially mustn't be held responsible for the results. Finally then, thanks to Emma Acosta, Elif Baba, Ike Balbus, Bob Barbera, John Berdell, David Bleeden, Natalia De Lima Bracarense, Natally Brookson, William Callison, Adriana Castrillon, Catherine Chaput, Ralph Cintron, Annie Cot, Claire Decoteau, Andy Denis, Claus Dierksmeier, Malte Dold, Madhu Dubey, Mia Mihic Engelmann, Sébastien Engelmann, Sam Fleischacker, Rachel Forgash, Marco Guidi, Santhi Hejeebu, Begum Icelliler, Ali Khan, Erich von Klosst-Dohna, Tony Laden, Deirdre McCloskey, Sophia Mihic, Nadine Naber, Hayley Negrin, Joe Persky, Maureen Heffern Ponicki, Malcolm Quinn, Michael Quinn, Chris Riley, Eric Schliesser, Abe Singer, Jeff Sklansky, Will Small, David Stovall, Kim Wheatley, Daniel Williams, and Tahira Zainulabideen.

1

Introduction

Rationality has a distinctive meaning in economics. Although economists have never quite agreed on what rationality is, they have converged for the most part on a technical definition for their teaching and research. The core idea is that the rational economic actor, for example a producing firm, or a consuming household, chooses to get what it defines as more for less, rather than to get less for more (which would be irrational). Defender of economics Lionel Robbins wrote that economics is "the science which studies human behavior as a relationship between ends and scarce means which have alternative uses."[1] Critic Karl Polanyi wrote that economics "refers to a definite situation of choice, namely, that between different uses of means induced by an insufficiency of those means."[2] Once one turns one's attention to this situation of choice, one realizes that any economic unit can make a rational choice by doing a better rather than a worse job of using the means at its disposal. To choose rationally is to choose what will yield more of what one considers benefit and suffer less of what one considers cost.

There are many other philosophical and common-sense ways to think about what is rational or reasonable. Here are just a few: Reason is what distinguishes a valid from an invalid argument. Reason is what distinguishes a consistent or coherent from an inconsistent or incoherent account. Reason is a process or mode involved in figuring out how to solve a puzzle, or figuring out how to build something from scratch, or figuring out how to fix something that is broken. Reason guides one to do the right thing. Reason is a social process, or a procedure, for people to do things like reach compromise or take advantage of the fact that many heads are better than one. To be reasonable is to be receptive and consistent, as opposed to rigid and arbitrary. Reason is what broadly distinguishes enlightenment or true religion from ignorance or superstition. Reason is a challenge to domination, or reason is a mask for domination. Reason is low cunning, or reason is high dispensation. Economic rationality overlaps with some of these and others but it is quite specific. Whether we speak of a part or a unit, or an individual or a collective, to be economically rational is to behave or act in such a way as to yield more benefits, suffer fewer costs, or both, of any kind, as determined by preferences and their satisfaction under given constraints. Economic rationality always looks to the future, and that future can present itself as alternative scenarios likely to result from more or less rational choices: more or less rational, that is, given preferences and given limited means to satisfy those preferences.[3] Rationality, in an economic sense, is about allocative choice. The need to choose how to allocate is conditioned by scarcity. Economics points out, for example, that you only have so much time to do the things you want to do in this day, in this week, in this lifetime. How are you going to budget that time?

For most economists, one advantage of their approach to rationality is that it appears to be "value-free," unlike many of the alternatives listed above. Most critics agree, but they see this amorality as a vice. After all, the sinner might be just as rational, in an economic sense, as the saint, and both as rational as the prudent householder. Economic rationality on the dominant understanding is simply a vehicle one uses to take one, by the best route, wherever one wants to go. It does not seem to privilege any one way of life over another. Thus its more thoughtful defenders will point out that economic rationality flourishes in and is particularly appropriate to modern, complex, liberal societies, where people are rightly understood to have a plurality of ends, and a plurality of conceptions of the good life.

But economics cannot escape values any more than any other social science discipline can. As the American economist Frank Knight observed almost a century ago, economists are part of the social life that is their subject matter.⁴ Social life is made up of how people and things relate to one another; it is made up of what people do and how they talk about what they do. Economists are people too, and when they write and teach they necessarily affect the social life that they write and teach about. Their doing so isn't a problem – it's not some matter of personal "bias" getting in the way – it is instead how even or especially the most rigorous social science is done. Knight was the undergraduate and graduate teacher of several very prominent twentieth-century economists, including leading lights of the postwar American Right. Few would claim that *their* scientific practice left the world they studied unchanged.

Both defenders and detractors say that economic rationality selects means for given ends, that it is simply "instrumental." But that's not strictly speaking true. Instead, allocative choice means that ends are "traded off" with one another in light of the chooser's limited means; they are rendered commensurable, or somehow comparable, on a single scale. Do you want to read this book right now? How does it compare with something else you might be doing? You can't do both! (Or can you? What about those people at gyms reading on the StairMaster™?) Critics are right that something is seriously awry with thinking of allocative choice as a model for rational action, that the deployment of economic rationality can obscure and even transform relations that work according to other logics. But these critics and even the most stalwart defenders are insufficiently appreciative of the rich political history and meaning of economists' way of reasoning. Economic reason was once couched in a broader political theory that charted a clear-sighted course in opposition to dependence on, and domination by, aristocrats and churchmen. It worked as one department of a new democratic art and science of government. Today, however, economic rationality disenchants politics,⁵ and thus degrades responses to domination and other problems of the commons.

To behave in an economically rational way is to do more with less, or get more from less. To be more rational in this way is to economize, to make better use of what is available, whatever one's aims. Economy, or economic efficiency, yields utility: whatever counts as satisfaction of priorities or preferences for and from any individual or collective conduct. Efficiency fights waste: that which could have been yielded but wasn't, because of a correctable problem of misallocation. If that's how economic rationality guides us, says the economist, it seems there is some kind of ethics or politics involved here after all: an opposition to waste no matter what one's purposes, with waste defined strictly in accordance with those purposes. What could be wrong with that?

To make better use of what is available is to exploit. Critics target this exploitation. Consider that colonists over the centuries have seized indigenous lands and the very bodies of colonized individuals, justified in part by metrics claiming more efficient use than the colonized were making without their presence. This new use was seen as more pleasing to God and because, without being dispossessed or enslaved, the indigenous would, according to the metrics, remain in a state of underdevelopment, in everyone's interest. Consider that employers devise ingenious ways to get more out of employees in often despotic workplaces in the name of the contribution this makes to the health of the competitive firm, and to the prosperity of the economy as a whole, even as aggregate metrics of prosperity can efface effects on workers, often including whether they even share in this prosperity at all. Consider that economic prosperity gained by efficiency unconsciously exploits and often disrupts or reshuffles an invisible array of care work, some of it in the paid labor force, so partly accounted for by economic measures, but much of it not. Care work becomes more visible in times of crisis: essential work that is shirked by most men and by people of higher status and is primarily done by women and immigrants and members of other subaltern groups. And, consider that humans generally dominate, or attempt to dominate, other animals and the rest of nature, exploiting them for their own purposes. Humans don't even dominate nature efficiently, from another point of view, if losses from pollution, or in fresh water, habitat destruction, extinction, heightened disease risk, and outright climate catastrophe, aren't even priced as costs.

Defenders of economic rationality will point to this last possibility, the possibility of newly recognizing and revising estimates of the benefits and costs of our actions, in order to showcase the enormous flexibility and indispensability of their framework. All material culture amounts to exploitation in some form, much of it surely either innocuous or reducing of harm. If our aim is to expose and to confront all forms of unjust and otherwise problematic use and abuse, so be it! We will still need to do that rationally as opposed to irrationally; we will still want to oppose this exploitation as economically as possible. If the critics are concerned that economic rationality turns everything and everyone into an instrument for use, the defenders of economic rationality will point out that it itself is an instrument for use. It still is a vehicle to take us where we want to go, wherever that is. By helping us to map out the most direct route to our destination economic rationality is, according to this retort, fundamental to individual and collective progress, whatever the standard or measure of progress might be.

The modern social-theoretical debate over economic reason – the fierce and overlapping anticolonial, critical race, socialist, feminist, and ecological attacks sketched above, and various responses to them from the liberal mainstream – goes back in its systematic form at least to Karl Marx's nineteenth-century critique of political economy. Marx disputed classical political economy's conception of capital. Capital for Marx is not, as political economy generally thought, dead labor serving living labor, but instead living labor serving dead labor. And economic rationality as we know it and currently live it – the push to do more with less, to find the higher return, to maximize the satisfaction of preferences no matter what those preferences are – is the logic of capital. Capital is a become-alien monster of our own creation, an insatiable vampire feeding off the living, and economic rationality is its drive. The capitalist is merely a "conscious bearer [*Träger*] of this movement."[6] Thus agents don't so much have (or not have) rationality: economic rationality, on the contrary, has them. In the twentieth century Karl Polanyi put an ecological twist on this critique. Economic rationality on his view was the logic of the "disembedded" market, attacking the foundations of the societies in which it needed to be re-embedded for its own and our very survival, and provoking counter-movements of the self-defense of society in response. Economic rationality sets itself upon its very preconditions. Whether one understands those preconditions as the treasures of the earth, the treasures of long-accreted or flexible and inventive human relations and human potential, or the treasures of the very institutions – law, property, money, etc. – that it functionally requires, economic rationality, left to itself, eats its seed corn.[7]

Marx and Polanyi, as well as a complex of decolonial/feminist/ecological approaches, are not launching "normative" critiques of economics so much as they are refusing its dominant descriptions and explanations as being incomplete or misleading, and substituting others. In fact, the misconception some economists have that their critics are moralizers goes hand in glove with the misconception that some non-economists have, that economists are immoralizers, supposedly pushing the idea that people are just out for themselves. That said, modern critical-theoretical concerns are powerfully resonant with older, and still very active, traditions of moral criticism of economic rationality and economic thinking. Generations of moralists of various stripes have worried about the problems that economic rationality poses for the ethical individual. If your aim is to realize your preferences as efficiently as possible, no matter how unselfish those preferences might be, what does this mean for your fundamental duties? A commitment cannot really be a commitment, a duty can't truly be a duty, if it can be dislodged and traded off as just another value or preference to be weighed against other values or preferences.[8]

Consider the promise. In the English seventeenth century, to break a promise was to dishonor yourself and dishonor God. In the twenty-first-century US, law schools treat corporate contracts only as seriously as the cost of violating them ("reputational cost" does not capture what it is to lose honor). Regardless of how much or how little promise-breaking is punished, or promise-keeping rewarded, by law or norm, your promise to someone isn't really a promise if you make it thinking you'll keep it only so long as from your point of view the beneficial (in any sense, for anyone or anything you care about, which could even be that someone) consequences of doing so outweigh the costs. Being ready to treat such matters – one's relation with another, one's own decided practice – as so much "sunk cost" in the face of a new landscape of threat or opportunity, seems to involve an *akrasia* or weakness of the will, where your resolve is ever-susceptible, and your conduct vulnerable, to new temptations or their equivalents. Or maybe it's the opposite. Maybe your will is strong, even monstrously so, in your careful calculation of the benefits from a change of course and your readiness and willingness to move away, at the drop of a hat, from past patterns.

Questions or problems of independence and self-command are intimately tied up with the history of economic rationality. To tell some of that history is to show how economics is moral and political from the beginning. My main concern about the limits of social-theoretical and ethical critiques is that they might take economics too much at its word, that it doesn't do ethics and politics, and not recognize how, even after the loss of the "political" in political economy, economic rationality does its political work. As a matter of fact, it is more able to do the political work it now does *because* it is free of its classical moorings. That freeing allowed a new foundation in allocative choice. Once this introspective or psychic (if not psychological) vision was triumphant, economic rationality was free gradually to colonize or displace existing modes of political sovereignty.

Allocative choice and its political entailments are only reinforced by the recent challenge to rationality from within economics. Behavioral economists informed by cognitive psychology propose an alternative to the rationality assumption in systematic irrationality: for example, the tendency for economic actors consistently to underestimate distant costs and benefits in comparison to near ones. On the one hand, behavioralists participate in the myth that economics is a value-free science. On the other hand, they bring to the surface, through their practice, economic rationality's buried historical and conceptual connections to an art and science of government animated by a kind of utilitarian evangelism. Behavioral economists view humanity as fallen, as "crooked timber," and they are spreading the news while doing their best to help. Straightening us out is impossible, and thus a body of research works to inform policy that nudges us toward more rational behavior, and thus makes our crookedness less damaging to ourselves than it now is. In their narrow diagnostic and therapeutic approach, behavioralists run the risk of cementing varieties of contemporary servitude by arguing that our problems are of a cognitive rather than political cast, and then treating them as such. Think, for example, how different it is to approach retirement security as a problem for better systems-design fostering better individual decisions, rather than engage a collective struggle for pension rights.

In this book I excavate the political theory of economic rationality. It contrasts with the political theory of classical political economy, which targeted lordship as part of an emerging democratic art of government. Political economy mutated and buried its political theory when it built a new foundation on *choice*. Economics' dominant political theory treats social and political space as a classless, dynamic space of unaffiliated choosers. It aims to govern economic actors as harmoniously as possible *through* the choices they make, and to educate, adjust incentives, or resort to carefully chosen administrative fiat when those choices go seriously awry. Thus the turn of behavioral economics to psychological science and managerial technique merely makes explicit the implicit governmental logic of the postclassical turn. But the people who either tamed or threw off the old aristocracy didn't do so through individual or even policy choices. They, that is, those who saw a problem at all, saw the problem of aristocracy as a problem affecting them differently but common to them, a problem that, like all entrenched common problems, could ultimately only effectively be addressed by way of self-organization and collective action.

What follows is about an open secret: economics is an art and science of government. If we had any doubt – despite the economics-educated staff, think-tanks, and firms guiding states and corporations, and despite the rise of personal finance and related choice-aids even for households of modest means – behavioral economists have dispelled it with their public and private sector reforms designed to help people act better. Most economists will sincerely protest that theirs is not a political science, and not nearly so consequential. They think that if their work is practical at all they only serve, and that no one really listens to them anyway. Moreover, many will say, behavioral colleagues are outliers in their questioning of agents' rationality and in their meddling policy ambitions. Behavioral economists are instead, however, reminders of the discipline's roots as a moral science, specifically a secular evangelical project that promoted particular virtues toward the reform of individual and collective life. At the same time, behavioral economists' reliance on cognitive psychology reflects how far the discipline has traveled from its roots as a self-consciously social and political science. The irony of behavioral economics is that its attacks on economic rationality as a description of, or stylized model of, behavior are about reinforcing economic rationality as a prescription for and governor of behavior. The refinement and reproduction of a particular idea of rationality has been the refinement and reproduction of the administrative logic that animates economic theory and practice. Political economy once engaged with other literatures to promote egalitarian self-command and democratic reform; economics has increasingly turned away from the rest of the humanities to promote better individual and institutional choice.

My argument proceeds in three stages. First (Chapter 2), I guide the reader through a basic introduction to textbook rationality and the behavioral challenge, and situate both in the recent history of the discipline. Rationality is less descriptive or heuristic and more prescriptive. Rational or not, allocative choice is a weird way to do things, and its weirdness involves an abstraction from relations between economic agents, and between them and their choices and the things they choose. Framing action in the introductory textbook way doesn't just leave agents in charge and their ends untouched. Instead, by rendering ends commensurable, the framing allows less for considered action than it does for predictable reaction, and the behavioral critique reinforces said framework. Second (Chapter 3), I revisit classical political economy. Like other critics I go back to Adam Smith, but less for his classical ethics and more for the quasi-republican politics with which those ethics are entangled. Smith was concerned about liberty and domination, and the virtues needed to sustain the first and avoid the second. Although these concerns were blunted, in political economy proper, by the full turn to happiness in the nineteenth century, they certainly didn't disappear: the critique of domination is, if anything, more on the surface in the canonical, virtue-forward work of John Stuart Mill than it is in Smith. Third (Chapter 4), I do a close reading of Lionel Robbins' foundational essay in economic theory. With reference back to Robbins' fellow Englishmen William Stanley Jevons and Philip Wicksteed, and forward to the American Gary Becker, I make the case that Robbins' deliberately vague and ultimately consensual "harmony" definition of economic rationality (it is neutral between competing conceptions in the literature) is not the value-free project he presents it as but, instead, a highly consequential brief for the sovereignty of his science and its work. Robbins' approach set up economics as an indispensable expertise, providing internal justification for its increasing institutional presence and power through the twentieth century and beyond. Jeremy Bentham, critic of Smith on usury, mentor to Mill, and inspiration for the choice (as frame and foundation) turn in Anglophone economics, figures in both Chapters 3 and 4, a reminder that both post-Smithian political economy and economics are projects, however stunted, of a utilitarian art and science of government. (Bentham's importance to the tradition was once well understood, but it has since been obscured and is here restored.) As a look back at selected major figures these chapters resemble a brief history of "economy" – perhaps *the* foundational concept in economics – with all the strengths and weaknesses of that approach. But they, and the chapter preceding, are less history of economics than attempts to read economics and its rationality as political theory, attempts to bring out the political theory that is embedded there.

If Marx was right, then economic rationality should be understood more as force than frame. And, certainly, no amount of re-framing is going to help with next month's rent or next month's payroll: it won't make any individual or organization less subject to economic imperatives and thus to rationality's prescriptions. But this book is written with the wager that it is worth alerting readers to, or reminding them of, the political and ethical costs and consequences of the microeconomic mode.[9] It's worth remembering too that the mainstream tradition of political economy and its broader classical utilitarianism are themselves a potential source of alternative, that is, non-microeconomic, approaches to the problems of individual and collective government. These can at least inspire counterforces to economic rationality, and perhaps much more. As I argue in the Conclusion, the political theory of choice economics is, by contrast, particularly ill-suited to contend with multiple crises. To the extent that economics has performatively disenchanted all politics but its own, it is time to re-enliven other political perspectives and possibilities, to be more aware of the primacy of the public, of the commons, and what it calls for.

My account, which tells one story about the emergence of a specific rationality in economics, makes modern economics, in a sense, into a branch of politics. There is a kind of tit for tat here. Many economists have been doing something along these lines to politics for decades now, making it into a branch of economics. But, whereas some of those economists claim to be able to explain all political problems in economic terms, I make no such claim about economic problems. I am not writing so much about economic problems as I am about the political work done by a particular kind of economics. The microeconomic mode makes both economic and political problems (and, really, any existential problem or puzzle at all) into matters, at base, of *choice* and *rationality*. Many economists think of the problems they study in other terms, and don't link them to these micro-foundations. What follows has little or nothing to do with them and their work.[10] But allocative choice is still the starting point for most introductions to the discipline. Chapter 2 turns to one such introduction, in the world's best-selling economics textbook.[11]

2
Textbook Rationality and the Behavioral Critique

Textbooks are especially important in economics. Since the earliest days of the discipline it is leading practitioners who have laid down basic orthodoxy in widely circulated texts. Jean-Baptiste Say, early in the nineteenth century, lamented that there was no "established textbook on the science of political economy," and wrote one that was adopted, according to its American editor, "in all the universities of the continent of Europe."[1] John Stuart Mill's *Principles of Political Economy* (1848) went through seven editions in his lifetime. Alfred Marshall's *Principles of Economics* (1890) went through eight. Examining today's textbook rationality and its disciplinary applications helps to establish whether rationality is descriptive of conduct, prescriptive for conduct, or an idealization or abstraction from conduct. Examining textbook rationality is the beginning of figuring out who, if anyone, is rational. Are some individuals or groups of people more rational than others? Are economists the rational ones, theorizing with a tool not shared by the rest of us? The investigation of textbook rationality helps to illuminate how broadly rationality is supposed to apply when ascribed by economists. Does the orthodox view see economic rationality as something that applies to all human activities, or only to activities narrowly concerned with profit, if even those?

Behavioral economists fiercely criticize the textbook view. I argue that both defenders of economic rationality and many critics, whether from within or outside economics, all misunderstand something important. They miss rationality's ethical and political substance and its radical history as a reforming art and science of government. I share the concerns of extra-disciplinary critics about the limits of economic rationality, its cost/benefit analysis, and what happens when those limits are traversed. But I think it valuable to explore the relationship between rationality and its limits, on the one hand, and a rich tradition of political economy on the other. Before exploring those limits and that tradition in more detail it is important to know just what "economic rationality" means in its standard presentation today. The barrage of recent behavioral criticism from within the field has been clarifying. Ironically, the behavioral assault has served only to reinforce its target. Economic rationality remains as abstracting and ambitious as ever. But now any more capacious art and science of government is further narrowed into an art and science of management, into a theory of incentives. Assaulted for its inadequacy as description, economics' idealization of rationality morphs into a kind of prescription, and behavioralists are standing by to fill it.

Choice, scarcity, and economic reason

Looking at introductory textbooks, one sees that economics today is all about *choice*. In fact, so much so that "choice" is often put in italics, as in the previous sentence. Here is a recent example:

> Is economics about money: How people make it and spend it? Is it about business, government, and jobs? Is it about why some people and some nations are rich and others poor? Economics is about all these things. But its core is the study of *choices* and their *consequences*.[2]

Mainstream economics studies what we call "the economy" in terms of patterns of interaction among a huge number of individual choices made by consuming households and producing firms. Choice is foundational for contemporary economics, and it is in and through choice that a distinctive idea of economic rationality comes into play.

What's meant by choice is quite mundane. For an economist, people are always making choices because they live in a condition of *scarcity*. "Scarce" is another word that often shows up in italics at the beginning of textbooks. The international bestseller of the postwar era, Paul Samuelson's *Economics*, puts scarcity alongside choice at the beginning of its definition of the discipline: "Economics is the study of how people and society end up *choosing*, with or without the use of money, to employ *scarce* productive resources that could have alternative uses....."[3] It is important to understand what economists mean by scarcity, a basic assumption of the field. Economists aren't saying that people don't have enough. Some might have plenty, but all live with scarcity. Scarcity simply means that there is a finite supply of something that could be useful: in principle, imagined or desired uses might have no limits. Many very rich people, for example, would like to have more time. For more than a few eccentrics the preference for more time extends to paying for the impossible (or at least not-yet-possible): having their bodies or just their brains frozen in the expectation that they might one day be revivable.[4]

But we don't have to reach for bizarre examples to get at what economists are saying. They are talking about everyday living, just from a certain point of view. Consider that if you are doing one thing, you're not doing any number of other things you might like to do. If I sit here writing, I'm not getting up and going to the fridge. If you take a shift at the call center, you're not reading this book. If you get takeout, you're not cooking at home. If I am taking care of my elderly parent, I'm not going out on a date. If you buy more groceries, you're not buying as much clothing. If I don't buy a house, I'll continue paying rent. If you buy more of one stock or bond, you're not buying as much of another. The list goes on. Some of my examples might seem more obviously economic than others. They are modern examples skewed to life in the "developed" world, but most economists think this logic applies anywhere, anytime, to the entirety of the human condition, and at least a few even think it applies well beyond the human.[5] These examples all ask: "how much of something do I give to this, and how much to that?" They are economic according to the Samuelson definition: they involve a problem of allocation, of choice under scarcity. Because of scarcity, the economist says, choice is inevitable. Rationality for the economist always applies to conduct understood as allocative choice. Note that one doesn't have to look at conduct from this point of view. One might not think of conduct in terms of choice at all (but in terms of habit, or necessity, or rule-following, or responsiveness, or drive, or craft, etc.), and if in terms of choice not in terms of allocative choice. One might think, for example, of simply choosing to do something, and choosing to do it in a particular way, because that's what one wants or needs to do right now, and that's the way to do it (for example, satisfying hunger by getting up and going to the fridge, which, assuming it's not empty, seems like a rational way to satisfy hunger).

Economic rationality is generally thought of as a kind of instrumental rationality, guiding one to choose certain means to given ends, whatever the ends are. After all, if your end is not your own enrichment but to help as many others as possible, the economist reminds you that if you help more rationally you can help more people. But there's something a bit obscure and under-theorized in a typical textbook definition of rationality. Consider the definition of "rational people" given in the leading introductory textbook of the twenty-first century, Gregory Mankiw's *Principles of Economics*. There, "**Rational people** systematically and purposefully do the best they can to achieve their objectives, given the available opportunities."[6] To understand this in purely instrumental terms, one might start with the objective or series of objectives that said people have, and then think of them accomplishing those objectives in the most effective way possible, as in my hunger/fridge example above. But that's not quite it; that's not all about allocation of scarce means. For the genuinely instrumental actor, what is relevant above all is that things get done (the mission accomplished, the problem solved, the service delivered, etc.). That wouldn't, however, be thinking like an economist.

If your objective is to clear everyone out of a building because you see a fire, the instrumentally rational thing to do is to pull the fire alarm before exiting; if you simply shout "Fire, Fire!" repeatedly on the way out of the door, many people may not hear you, and you will likely be less effective in accomplishing the objective. If I have two primary objectives in mind, say to commit a murder *and* not get caught, I am instrumentally rational if I think about not only how to kill my victim effectively but also how to cover my tracks effectively. The need to accomplish both objectives is reflected in my choice of methods. Perhaps I'm a chemist, and whipping up a poison would be easy. But everyone knows that chemists know a lot about poison, which would point the finger at me. So, unless I can concoct a poison that won't leave a trace, I choose another way to kill.

The "systematically" in Mankiw's definition of rationality, and the ambiguity of "best they can" – rational people "systematically and purposefully do the best they can to achieve their objectives" – give us a clue that we haven't understood his definition if pure instrumental effectiveness in accomplishing one's ends with available means (one way of reading "given the available opportunities") is our guide. Mankiw doesn't mean that a rational person just sets out to accomplish certain things. The ten principles of economics listed in the first chapter of the book suggest otherwise. Mankiw groups the first four principles under the heading "How People Make Decisions." The first of these reminds the reader that choice, for the economist, is always choice under scarcity: "People Face Trade-Offs."[7] Mankiw models all decision-making as allocative choice, where more of this often means less of that. Thus, according to economists, rational decisions are made in the fuzzily expansive and aggregating language of *cost* and *benefit*, where everything is comparable with everything else, at least from the chooser's point of view.

All your various ends and means, likely including ends and means you haven't even thought of, are in consideration all the time, and any one of your objectives is subject to comparison and trade with any other, at any time. Economists mostly reject that your preferences can reasonably be weighed against mine, because we are two different people. But, even the fiercest disciplinary opponents of that weighing are confident that your appreciation of a sunset, for example, can be weighed against the pleasure you take in conversation with a loved one because, according to economists, you do this weighing all the time, as revealed through the choices you actually make. Whatever you do, through your own agency, you show the theorist of allocative choice what you have chosen to do, and what not to do. This can coherently extend well beyond market choices to your choices to pray, to give a gift, to respect standards of hygiene, you name it.

Mankiw's first principle directly implies the second, that you're not likely being economically rational if you simply consider the visible cost of doing something, because "The Cost of Something Is What You Give Up to Get It." When you trade off you always have an "opportunity cost" of not doing something else. Notice how far any such consideration potentially takes you from the instrumentally rational accomplishment of an objective. You are considering how much doing something costs, not just how best to do it. Let's go back to my murder plans. It turns out that they might not be worth doing, even if I have the means, because of any number of other lesser objectives I have. Thus for people to be "systematic" and do the "best they can" in relation to their objectives means to be globally *efficient*, but not necessarily instrumentally *effective* from the point of view of what was, after all, a primary objective. Murder might never happen, even though it is a high priority and I have the means to do it. How effective is that?

Yes, questions of effectiveness can and must be part of and folded into questions of efficiency; that's how I figured out that accomplishing a particular objective, at least for the time being, wasn't "worth it." But notice that I am ultimately thinking less of what an end, however bad or good that end, requires for its accomplishment, and more in terms of what I require for the accomplishment of my ends. My thinking is directed less to the world and its calls and possibilities, and more to me and my aims, however "selfless" those aims, and my possibilities. I need then to figure into the cost of any objective the aforementioned opportunity cost, the potential benefits neglected by doing this and not something else. Costs are not, therefore, simply what they appear to be. Mankiw reminds us that one can only know the true cost of a university education, for example, by adding to its tuition and fees the wages one could have made by working during that time instead.[8] It's with his third principle that Mankiw introduces the definition of "rational people," in the course of elaborating "Rational People Think at the Margin." Marginalism is a key feature of rationality as it is defined and formalized by economists.

The rational decision-maker must compare not just costs and benefits, but *marginal* costs and benefits, and choose the course where marginal benefits outweigh marginal costs. Mankiw gives a common textbook example: airlines and seat sales. An airline is going to fly a route regardless, even if the plane is not full. If a plane is ready to fly and there are seats remaining it might be profitable for the airline to sell those seats at a very low price. This is because each additional passenger costs the airline very little: the plane is already fully staffed, and the additional snacks and fuel consumed because of an added passenger are very small at the margins. The textbook, which is a bit out of touch in this regard, references cheap standby tickets, now largely a thing of the past, but standby is still the way for airline employees to hitch a ride at little cost to the airline.[9] The idea is that airline executives make a mistake if they think of the total cost per passenger of flying and calculate costs and thus prices that way because what counts, if the plane is going to fly regardless, is the marginal cost of each additional passenger. Conversely, the marginal benefit over cost from an additional passenger paying a standard fare gets quite high as the plane approaches capacity. Airlines have discovered that, at least in normal times, empty seats might seem to be cheap but represent significant opportunity costs, and so they commonly overbook.

For households and firms, marginalism means that getting choice right can involve a lot of fine-tuning. "Rational people know that decisions in life are rarely black and white [the marginal theorist actually posits, wrongly, that they are never black and white] but often involve shades of gray."[10] Thinking at the margin means being misled if the "more and less" involved in rational tradeoffs is made about the thing or stuff itself rather than about particular increments of things and stuff: the tenth dollar, the twentieth banana, the second hour, etc. Your household might like bananas very much, but you can only enjoy so many each day, and your enjoyment of each added banana declines. If you have more bananas than you can possibly eat or preserve, then the extra bananas, which will only spoil, aren't worth anything to you at all. Mankiw doesn't mention it here, but margins are why "sunk cost" thinking is economically irrational. If you think in terms of absolute rather than marginal costs and benefits you can make big mistakes. You'll think in terms of how much time you have spent on an unrealized project, or how much money you have spent, and perhaps think that this is a reason why you need to continue. But the question you need to ask is how much *additional* time or money remains to be spent and whether what it will bring is worth it. Economic rationality always looks forward, always looks to the future.

The discussion of rationality and marginalism leads to the fourth and final principle of "How People Make Decisions": "People Respond to Incentives."[11] This principle in turn provides a crucial bridge between the apparently isolated choices of economic actors in relation to all their objectives and budgets, and the discussion of six remaining principles of economic *interaction* and the aggregate effects that flow from it. Incentives generally come from others, and the price system is a giant incentive machine.[12] Economic rationality stipulates that, other things being equal, people will adjust their behavior predictably when prices rise or fall: rising prices in the market for widgets will incentivize consumers to cut back and find substitutes, and will incentivize producers to make more widgets. This is the secret of markets' remarkable capacity to organize decentralized decision-making. The capacity was ennobled by the twentieth-century Austrian theorist Friedrich Hayek, who, in a twist on the classical critique of the limits of the knowledge of political authorities, described this process as a wonderfully spontaneous one, which effectively exploits dispersed intelligences and in this way and others is much more far-sighted and nimble than any central planner could possibly be.[13] Economists say that markets work as they ideally should when all the players are "price takers" rather than "price makers," responding to the market and in this way equilibrating, through their choices under scarcity, the supply of goods and services with the demand for them. Mankiw's remaining principles, which cover "How People Interact" and "How the Economy as a Whole Works," and the chapter as a whole, both argue for the superiority of market coordination, while allowing that "government action can potentially improve market outcomes."[14] He chides "public policymakers" always to keep incentives in mind, or face unintended consequences of government attempts to shape decision-making.[15]

Mankiw's introductory sketch of rationality in individual decision-making provides the basis for a later and more advanced discussion of the theory of consumer choice. Keep in mind for now the pivot from action to interaction, with incentive as a bridge between them. It is not yet clear whether this is to be taken as descriptive of anyone's behavior, or if it is a prescription: some way in which one must or should behave. Perhaps it is neither but instead a kind of working definition or basic model for the purposes of doing economic science, one that only needs the kind of confirmation it gets from the study of specific markets. If economic rationality is a model, is a kind of disciplinary idealization, is something that makes salient certain aspects of the human condition and allows others to recede into the background, then that idealization perhaps models not so much action as reaction. To be a genuine economic actor, it seems, is to be responsive to incentives.

Economic rationality and economic science

Mankiw hasn't given much of a hint about either how descriptive rationality is supposed to be, or how wide the range of people or things or activities it might describe. In his examples he moves quickly to choices that can be "costed out" in terms of categories like time and money, both of which as metrical commonplaces are peculiarly modern social technologies, or at least technologies that have a distinctively modern form. Mechanical clock time that gives us regular intervals of hours, for example, didn't exist until the medieval era.[16]

When Mankiw moves from his first four principles to the remaining six he introduces familiar ideas from mainstream economics: free trade and comparative advantage, the invisible hand and the general superiority of market organization, market failures and the capacity for public policy to enhance efficiency and equality (along with warnings about the political process), productivity growth as the secret of rising living standards, the money supply and the relationship between excess supply and inflation, and trade-offs between inflation and unemployment.[17] The textbook has remarkably little to say about economic crises in the wake of the global crash of 2008; it treats the crash, when it does at all, as neatly contained in space (the US) and time ("the great recession of 2008–2009").[18] It contrasts in this and many other respects with Samuelson's twentieth-century classic, whose "mixed economy" perspective was shaped from beginning to end by the experience of the Great Depression.

The core idea of weighing consequences at the heart of economic rationality is very old. And it has certainly always had a prominent place in the history of political economy. Most historians would say that it was not moved to the very center of the discipline – it was not made foundational in the way Mankiw does in his textbook – until at least the marginal or "neoclassical" revolution of the latter part of the nineteenth century, which put the individual producer/consumer and their valuing choices at the heart of the project of understanding the social processes that we label "economic." And it should be said that many working economists since the revolution have departed from the tendency to make economic rationality so central. But these controversies have been less about economic rationality per se than about its role in understanding economic processes.

Mankiw, at least for the purposes of an introductory textbook, makes rationality foundational and ties it directly to a series of aggregate effects. For classical political economy something like economic rationality was more a byproduct of particular social and political arrangements. Late nineteenth- and early twentieth-century "institutionalists" and their successors have taken up and further developed this insight; for many of them, understanding these arrangements and the conflicting class or group interests that haunt or sustain or advance them should be the primary work of economists.[19] And in the wake of the Great Depression John Maynard Keynes would famously strike at the heart of neoclassical economics, as perhaps only a former believer could, by suggesting that its story connecting rational microfoundations to efficient economic processes fails to face up to reality. It does not allow for the possibility of involuntary unemployment, and yet involuntary unemployment and underemployment are all around us. Traditional theory is limited in its usefulness to the special case of full employment. Keynes's implication is that much of the time the aggregate effects of individually rational decisions, left to themselves, will lead to disaster.[20]

Keynes and his heirs launched a new perspective that would cast aside or at least de-center the rationalist foundation, and that would generate a new field of "macroeconomics" and a new role for economists as disinterested managers of a capitalist system otherwise prone to crisis.[21] Heterodox critics (e.g. Austrians and Marxists) in turn objected to this Keynesian management from opposite ends of the disciplinary-political spectrum, agreeing with one another that it was anything but disinterested. Samuelson and his allies in the profession rehabilitated economic rationality as a foundation, but in their modified Keynesianism they produced the familiar textbook perspective that lives on in Mankiw's more market-friendly treatment. What is this textbook perspective on the role and function of economic science? For a long time now the mainstream of the profession has been largely in agreement that rational choice provides the foundation for economic analysis, but economists are attuned from the get-go to the many failures of markets to maximize efficiency, and to policy's role in mitigating those failures. It is evident that Mankiw, along with numerous others, shares elements of the critique of this professional consensus, even as the Samuelsonian orientation lives on in his treatment. For Mankiw the disinterested economist is still an adviser to governments attuned to market failure, but this economist is a critic of the state as well as of society, and not just a critic of the limits of state knowledge. Mankiw's position attests to the influence of the neoliberal[22] "public choice" school of what he calls "political economy," defined in his text as a science that "uses the methods of economics to study how government works."[23] Such an application thinks of public officials as self-interested actors even in the performance of their official acts. In its presumption that duties of office are essentially private matters, and that all such matters are somehow commensurable and subject to tradeoff, the perspective assumes, in a word, corruption;[24]

so the idea might be to eliminate or modify state functions simply to reduce the opportunities for corruption.

The Samuelsonian postwar consensus suggests that economics has become a *policy* science.[25] This orientation is evident in textbooks, but it is also evident in the formal admission of economics to government in institutions such as the US president's Council of Economic Advisors, not to mention the importance of economists in the myriad think-tanks and other non-governmental organizations that have come to populate the modern policy landscape. That economics is now a policy science applies just as much to Mankiw's neoliberalism as it did to Samuelson's neo-Keynesianism. It applies just as much to Washington's market-libertarian Cato Institute as it does to Washington's labor-founded Economic Policy Institute. Samuelson's textbook makes the connection explicit early on: "Ultimately, understanding should aid in *control and improvement*." The textbook immediately connects improvement not to a statement of values, not to tell us what improvement "looks like from an economist's point of view, but to a statement of instrumental value-freedom, a statement of the neutrality and objectivity of economic science. "We know that a doctor passionately interested in stamping out disease must first train himself to observe things as they are. His bacteriology cannot be different from that of a mad scientist out to destroy mankind."[26] This medical analogy, and the connection it suggests between the art of government and the science of society, was popular among the utilitarian philosophers of social reform whose work inspired the formation of disciplines of social science, including economics, in the nineteenth century. But notice how it subtly extends whatever might exist in the way of scientific consensus to imply a non-existent political consensus about what a good society looks like. G. K. Chesterton's objection remains as relevant today as it did over one hundred years ago: "(t)he social case is exactly the opposite of the medical case. We do not disagree, like doctors, about the precise nature of the illness, while agreeing about the nature of health."[27]

Mankiw seems initially to want to draw a bright line between science and policy. In his second chapter, "Thinking like an Economist," he writes the following: "When economists are trying to explain the world, they are scientists. When they are helping improve it, they are policy advisers." But notice that the goal of improvement is taken for granted: there is no mention of destructive mad scientists here. And it is never clear why or how a statement such as "if substitutes are available higher prices for a good will tend to suppress demand for it" becomes any less scientific when stated in the course of a policy discussion. The distinction between science and policy is made to distinguish "positive" from "normative" statements: "In general, statements about the world come in two types ... **Positive statements** are descriptive. They make a claim about how the world *is* ... **Normative statements** are prescriptive. They make a claim about how the world *ought to be*."[28] Is economists' idea of rationality positive or normative, or something else? Recall that Mankiw's four principles from his first chapter covered "How People Make Decisions." That people make choices in the face of scarcity, and thus face trade-offs, would seem to be a statement about how the world is. When introducing and defining rationality in the course of introducing marginal thinking, Mankiw writes: "Economists normally assume that people are rational."[29]

Whatever its status as a scientific assumption, economic rationality in Mankiw's use is closely tied to an art. But this art is not, directly at least, the art of public policy. Recall that rational people "systematically and purposefully do the best they can to achieve their objectives, given the available opportunities." Economic rationality is crucial, it seems, to the improvement of people's everyday living, just as economic science is crucial to the improvement of the world in which people live. But does this mean all aspects of everyday living? If we turn back to Samuelson, we see a discussion late in his text of what was in the 1970s thought of as "the new microeconomics." The discussion opens by saying that it "used to be thought that economics deals only with goods and services that lend themselves to the measuring rod of money and market pricing," and it then alerts us to research on the economics of time, "human capital," population, law, and even "love and altruism."[30] The application of economic rationality well beyond money and market pricing to discrimination, crime and punishment, education, family life, etc.

is usually associated with the pandisciplinary ambitions of "peak rationality" Chicago-school economist Gary Becker. Becker received the Nobel Prize in Economics in 1992 "for having extended the domain of microeconomic analysis to a wide range of human behavior and interaction, including non-market behavior."[31]

Pace Samuelson and the Nobel committee, however, Becker was successfully formalizing a return of "microeconomic analysis" to its roots. Consider the English economist Philip Wicksteed, who in *The Common Sense of Political Economy* (1910) writes the following:

> In the ordinary course of our lives we constantly consider how our time, our energy, or our money shall be spent. That is to say, we decide between alternative applications of our resources of every kind, and endeavour to administer them to the best advantage in securing the accomplishment of our purposes or the humouring of our inclinations ... It follows that the general principles which regulate our conduct in business are identical with those which regulate our deliberations, our selections between alternatives, and our decisions, in all other branches of life ... The art of life includes the art of effectively and economically distributing our vital resources of every kind ... If we secure this, how much of that must we pay for it, or what shall we sacrifice to it? And is it worth it? What alternatives shall we forgo? And what would be their value to us?[32]

Economic policy as identified by Samuelson suggests the role of economic science in a kind of social therapeutics, in the form of advising public policy in the cause of quasi-medical improvement. In Wicksteed the economic rationality at the heart of economic science is also fundamental to *individual* therapeutics, in the form of help in using one's "vital resources" well. And perhaps this is not surprising, when one considers that for the economic mainstream, at least, the way to think about society and social decisions is as an aggregate of individual decision-making. Much remains obscure in these connections, however, as does much about the positive or normative status of statements about rationality. Mankiw winds down the micro part of his text where he began, with choice, by illustrating some of the complexities of a theory of consumer behavior. He explicitly speaks of "optimization" of the satisfaction of preferences or, in an alternative language, the goal to "maximize utility," to describe what it is to achieve objectives systematically and purposefully as best one can. And this, along with Wicksteed's language of constant consideration, raises the question of what kind of practice this optimizing or maximizing is.[33]

The philosopher Anthony Laden usefully distinguishes between "episodic" and "ongoing" action. Episodic actions are temporally well defined; they have a beginning and an end and they involve an agent transforming some aspect of a world external to them.[34] It would seem at first blush that an optimal choice is the epitome of the episodic. Yet economic rationality suggests something that is in important respects ongoing, and that in its choices might have more of a reactive than active relationship to its surroundings: it responds to incentives. Maximizing utility is not really an action at all so much as a kind of continuing activity, a governor and guide to all an agent's actions which, even if transformative of an environment, might partake more of reaction than action.

Mankiw assumes rational allocative choice everywhere in an economy: producing firms as well as consuming households operate this way, even as they are relegated to separate discussions. The attribution of economic rationality without much qualitative distinction among market players is common practice in much modern economics. Note how different this is from Adam Smith's eighteenth-century perspective. Even as many of his assumptions were strikingly egalitarian, Smith distinguished among the three great classes of his time: the owners of land who live by rents, the owners of capital who live by profits, and the owners of labor who live by wages. Only the "merchants and dealers," as Smith called those who live by profit, were thought by him to see their interests accurately on a regular basis. Given freedom in a "system of natural liberty" they pursue their interests efficiently in a way that is beneficial to all, but, more than other classes, if this freedom extends to acquiring political power their use of that power may bring society to ruin.[35] In addition to applying to everyone, economic rationality for

Mankiw seems to apply to the full range of things that people do. Although more controversial, this in the wake of Becker is not unconventional. And it again contrasts with Smith, who would see the considerations appropriate to a bargain in trade as different from the considerations appropriate in politics or among friends; and even Smith's dealer's bargain, as a rhetorical act, looks very different from Mankiw's calculations. Who, if anyone, one might ask, actually abides by Wicksteed's "general principles which regulate our conduct in business"? Is optimizing rationality even true of people regularly involved in business transactions, much less other individuals? And are Wicksteed's principles appropriate for even business people beyond their business? What does it mean to translate everything into cost and benefit, even if the benefit is for others, and not directly for oneself? For now, we put these questions aside in order to engage a growing literature in contemporary economics that has questioned whether economic rationality is even at all descriptive of our conduct.

Allocative choice and the behavioral challenge

When he turns to an elaboration of the theory of consumer choice, Mankiw illustrates how household optimization works (a similar exercise for producing firms is performed earlier in the text). Here he writes of "budget constraints," the amount a consumer has to spend, and preferences and their "indifference curves," the graphing of bundles of goods that can be substituted for one another to provide equal levels of satisfaction. He writes of effects on choice of changes in income and changes in prices, and models these as well. All this allows for the graphing of "demand curves" for individual goods, showing the incentive effects on demand of changes in the price of a good, given the preceding analysis. This discussion – so far only about tradeoffs between pizza and Pepsi – is already quite complex for the layperson. Mankiw turns from it to a brief canvass of applications of the theory, including the interaction between wage rates and the allocation of time between work and leisure, and the interaction between interest rates and the allocation of income between present spending and saving. All of this takes into account the fact that people have different tastes for goods, for leisure, for present over future consumption or vice versa, and it takes into account a range of individual "income effects" and "substitution effects" (for example, does a fall in the price of a good improve one's bottom line or does one just buy more of the good?).[36] It is in a sidebar in the middle of the chapter that Mankiw discusses "Utility: An Alternative Way to Describe Preferences and Optimization."[37] He explains how the theory of consumer choice can be characterized as a theory of utility maximization. Does the prospect of two more liters of Pepsi provide one with as much expected utility, or overall satisfaction, as the prospect of one more pizza?

That even artificially stripped-down optimization or utility maximization is a complex business is clear from the mathematical literature on it. The reaction of Mankiw's reader is likely to be "this has nothing to do with how I make decisions about anything!" And he acknowledges this in his conclusion to the chapter titled "Do People Really Think This Way?" The answer to the question is "no." But it doesn't really matter. This is a scientific model and as such is "not intended to be completely realistic." More interestingly, the theory is a "metaphor for how consumers make decisions."[38]

Behavioral economics objects to the lack of descriptive realism in mainstream choice theory. Mankiw gives a sketch of behavioral economics in the next chapter, "Frontiers of Microeconomics."[39] The first frontiers, asymmetric information, or the problem that some parties to transactions are much better informed than others, and political economy, understood as the application of economics to politics, are both irreducibly concerned with interaction. The final frontier, behavioral economics, returns to the scene of choice with which we began, acknowledging that not only economics but "The social science of psychology also sheds light on the choices that people make in their lives."[40]

Behavioral economics objects to the rationality assumption as the basis of a positive science of economics. But, for decades, the positivist mainstream has insisted that the question of the realism of its assumptions is not relevant. In a highly influential article from the 1950s Milton Friedman maintained that it is only important that economic actors largely behave "as if" such calculations were being made, such that the discipline is able to generate hypotheses that can be tested to explain and predict economic phenomena.[41] Arguments over the years have generated a number of questions. Is rationality supposed to be a property of individuals, or is it a property of households and firms or even markets only? Is it not really even that, but instead a theoretical device or heuristic in the hands of the scientist only, at some remove from economic actors, yet still useful in understanding their aggregate activity?

Empirical objections to the neoclassical model and its variants are quite old. Institutionalists drew from other disciplines to question rationalist premises as any kind of foundation for the study of economic processes that were embedded in historically specific legal, social, and cultural formations. Learning from institutionalist challenges, Herbert Simon, who trained in political science but was a polymath student of organizations and pioneer in artificial intelligence, introduced "bounded rationality."[42] All economic actors, including the profit-making firms that Simon studied in some depth, engage not in utility-maximization abstractly understood but instead tend to demonstrate reasonable because "satisficing" behavior: they use procedures to realize aspirations in the face of limited information, time, and calculating power, and are satisfied when they have what suffices. Relatedly, actors might attack problems in importantly different ways; they use what psychologists and others would later call "frames" to shape their decision-making. Economic rationalists could absorb many of these ideas by turning satisficing, for example, into a kind of optimizing under conditions of uncertainty. They have made it all about "transaction costs," or the costs involved in such things as decision-making, and they point out that these too must be contained. In his Nobel lecture of 1978 Simon resists these appropriations.[43] And, despite his deep interest in and many contributions to cognitive science, it is clear that Simon's behavioral objections to economic rationalism are informed by several disciplines, and within psychology by more than one tradition of thought.

For Simon, "Bounded rationality is not irrationality."[44] His approach to rational decision-making is more genuinely instrumental than that modeled by economic rationality. It centers less on agents and more on their goals: more on agents' identifying and attending to the important problems and sorting out how to solve them and effectively implement solutions. Choosing correctly between a schedule of alternatives is by comparison a relatively minor affair. Here, of course, whether one is operating as part of a group or not is highly significant, and in either case there is an attention to better or worse decision *procedures*. Simon seems at times impressed and inspired by satisficing actors, rather than seeing them only in terms of their shortcomings by comparison with omniscient optimization; for example, study of the intuitive short-cuts that experts in any field take to categorize and address a problem informs advances in machine learning.[45]

Simon's work in these and other respects contrasts with contemporary behavioral economics. What is striking about the new behavioral economics is that it borrows entirely from psychology for its critique of the discipline. And in its turn to psychology it considers the mind exclusively from a cognitive point of view: less as a situated and developing entity and more as an independent information processor, like a computer, if a flawed one. This is ideal for applications to the scene of allocative choice. In his book *Misbehaving*, and in his Nobel lecture nearly forty years after Simon's, Richard Thaler credits developments in cognitive psychology with inspiring his work. Thaler answers the usual objections from rationalists by arguing that he has a theory of *systematic* cognitive bias in decision-making that is able to make more successful predictions than rationalists can. The behavioralists have slyly re-labeled what they too take to be an amoral or value-free optimizing rationality as "normative," and have studied in various subfields of economics how the normative predictions of the discipline often don't match its empirical findings. This has allowed them to substitute a systematic positive theory that generates hypotheses rooted in the gap between what rationality points to and what economic actors actually do. The theory is quite simple and elegant in this respect. Yes, economic processes come down to the people who conduct them, but those people are Humans, not Econs.

Through surveys and experiments and observation one can learn about many overlapping things common to human decision-making that don't make sense from an economist's point of view.

For example, humans see the difference between $4.99 and $5.00 as greater than the difference between $5.00 and $5.01. (We have left-digit bias.) If you ask me whether I'd drive to another store to save $10 on a $25 item I'd say "of course!" But if you ask me if I'd drive to another store to save $10 on a $1000 item I'd say "no way, not worth it." (The use of different frames makes us inconsistent in our calculations.) If you ask me whether I'd drive through a bad storm to get to an event I'd paid a lot for I would almost certainly do it, whereas if I had won the tickets I might well decline to go. (We care about sunk cost.) Maybe I keep a balance on a credit card and pay interest, even though I could pay off the card with savings that pay almost no interest. (We keep mental and other accounts that refuse the fungibility of money.) I would drink rather than conveniently sell a bottle of wine that had accrued in value, even though I'd never pay the new price for the same bottle. (We have loss aversion, valuing more what we have just because we have it.) I might applaud your taking a bowl of cashews out of the room rather than simply stop eating them or enjoying as many as I can. (We often lack self-control.) And I would spurn rather than accept an offer even if it would make me better off if I thought you were being unfair, just to deny you your share too. (We care about fairness and will pay to punish unfairness.)[46]

One of the peculiarities of behavioral economics is that it can lump together something like left-digit bias with something like a sense of justice, as if these are both quirks of the human mind. After all, one seems like a dispensable cognitive flaw not connected to much, like a simple matter of poor information processing, while the other seems much more than cognitive and bound up with a whole web of involvements, concerns, and characteristics. In fact, caring about fairness has long been thought essential to human living-together. (It's not even entirely clear from Thaler's account why this "bias," unlike left-digit bias, can't simply be incorporated into economic rationality, as a commonly found individual preference to be maximized along with others.) There is a story to be told about how certain kinds of passions, for example revenge, get written out of the history of political economy.[47] But for now simply consider the assumptions and implications of Thaler's approach. On the one hand, he clearly thinks that a world of Econs, the rational utility maximizers of mainstream theory, is impossible, and not a world that anyone would want to live in anyway. On the other hand, the flattening of these different so-called "anomalies," the way in which they are all put in a box together in terms of a common deviation from "normative" rationality, is telling.

Consider the place of economic rationality in the scheme. Behavioral economics conveniently brings to the surface an evangelism for prudent decision-making that has attached to political economy from its beginnings. On the one hand, Thaler and other behavioralists seem to think that the assumption of agents' rationality is a poor foundation for positive science. On the other hand, as Thaler puts it in his Nobel lecture, neoclassical theories "are essential … in characterizing optimal choices."[48] And this becomes extremely important for that substantial branch of behavioral economics that informs policy. The behavioralists view humanity as fallen. They work to inform policy that can guide us to be less damaging to ourselves, with our poor judgment and cognition, than we presently are. The reduction and attribution of social problems to a flawed psychology has gotten a huge boost amid the high-profile political-economic turmoil of recent years. In 2009 Thaler and law professor Cass Sunstein went so far as to pin the global financial crisis largely on cognitive shortcomings.[49] Their counterparts in political psychology point to similar shortcomings in their accounts of the rise of Brexit and Trump.[50] Readers are continually being told, in a host of books and papers, that they can't manage their own finances, much less democracy. Of course, good egalitarians that they are, many of the authors will let their audience know that as fellow humans they share the shortcomings they detail in others.

There is a hint in Thaler's work that fairness and loss aversion might not be in the same class as left-digit bias and might not be similarly irrational, but only a hint. Rationality for him remains what it is for Mankiw, the art of allocative choice that optimizes the satisfaction of a chooser's preferences, whatever those preferences might be. Thaler can reasonably maintain that the policy work he pioneered with Sunstein is not paternalist in the usual understanding. It constitutes a kind of "libertarian paternalism," not a contradiction in terms, because it preserves choice and imposes few costs. The insights of their highly influential *Nudge* are aimed at helping us to succeed in doing what we already prefer to do, or what we would at least endorse after the fact. *Nudge* rightly notes the existence of "choice architecture" all around us. From the arrangement of the food available in cafeterias to the designation of defaults in pension plans, we live with arrangements that guide us to more easily do one thing than another. To help us make optimal decisions, why not redesign those architectures in a way that better serves our welfare? The book is full of useful ideas. For example, make it so that people need to opt out of retirement saving in their workplaces rather than opt in, and in this way substantially augment their savings because of the inertia that behavioral economists call "status quo bias." What remains is a situation of choice, but a situation of choice more likely to realize the satisfaction of one's considered preferences. The *Nudge*-informed choice architect protects one from one's own worst tendencies, but in a way that fully preserves one's freedom to choose. In other words, nudges help humans better to optimize, better to maximize utility, in all kinds of circumstances where it is difficult for us at present to do so.[51]

As nudgers for economic rationality, then, behavioral critics only reinforce its sway. It is clear from their point of view that economic rationality is neither descriptive nor explanatory. What is it then, exactly? Because as idealization it shows the way, economic rationality is prescriptive, although each prescription is ostensibly one that an individual would willingly give themselves, if only they were capable on a regular basis of understanding and following it. Some nudges have a pedagogical quality. They help make humans into slightly better Econs. And, except for an occasional reference to a division between the "sophisticated" and the "unsophisticated," and an occasional nod to the impropriety of allocative choice in certain settings, behavioral economists continue and extend the modern tradition of applying (ir)rationality across populations and across spheres of life, well beyond the market. Ironically, then, behavioral critics are in these important respects economic rationality's fiercest defenders, or at least its most promising proselytizers.

In the course of reinforcing economic reason, behavioral economics, more importantly, reinforces the scene of choice with which introductory economics presents us. It raises the objection, however, that we tend to view this scene of choice through Human rather than Econ eyes. If Econs are pure creatures of incentive, Humans are cognitively limited creatures of habit such that incentives might not be salient to us. This does not mean, however, that incentives aren't relevant: quite the contrary. One mode of nudging is to increase their visibility: "good choice architects can take steps to direct people's attention to incentives."[52] Interactions on the behavioral view are still primarily and appropriately governed by signals according to which people adjust their conduct in an attempt to realize preferences. It is just that those signals are frequently misread, and, even if one properly reads them, one might have trouble weighing the costs and benefits, not to mention following through. The fundamental scene and "act" of allocative choosing remain intact.

Rationality, management, and politics

Choice under scarcity: according to textbook economists and their new behavioral critics it is from this scene that action, and then interaction, proceed. Anthropologists have long pointed out that what is so very strange about how economics models human interaction is not so much that it thinks in transactional terms, but that, as William Maurer puts it, "economists are always imagining that the end of transactions is to have them settled."[53] In fact, with the rise of "new institutionalist" work, the dominant way that economics has come to understand continuing relations (as opposed to one-off exchanges) is through its theory of transaction costs. It saves expense not to have to find new partners to contract with for every new endeavor, and so we settle into households and firms. The theory is intended to draw a sharp line between market and other transactions but, in order to understand these other transactions and the relations they inhabit, it models them as products of a continuing rational allocative choice. In some hands, then, the framework can simply blur the line it draws by, for example, treating internal commands as nothing but offers (would I rather be home by ten as my parent insists or quit this household? Would I rather write the memo the boss tells me to write or quit this job?).[54] And this in turn raises the question in the other direction, of how many market choices have the flavor of commands, once one reinforces the model of an economic actor as a creature of incentive. If in many market transactions people don't have the option not to choose because, for example, they are shopping for necessities, then what is apparently simply a good offer can take on the look and feel of command.

What does the anthropologists' objection mean, that economists think that the point of transactions is to have them settled? What this means is that an economist thinks the point of a decision that informs an exchange is whatever is exchanged and its relationship to the agent's preferences, whether those preferences are "egoistic," "altruistic," or somewhere in-between. Maurer's comment about economics was prompted by his interviewer's reference to a famous article in which an economist calls attention to the inefficiency of Christmas gifts, considering how often they don't maximize their recipients' utility.[55] They don't maximize the satisfaction of altruistic preferences that in the writer's view are the reason for the season. But what if the rituals and relations in which agents are embedded are prior to anyone's preferences? Behavioral economists could understand the differences between Humans and Econs in these terms, but they don't. Cognitive psychology as a frame gets in the way of such an understanding, because it treats relations as external to, rather than constitutive of, a predominantly information-processing decision-maker, however rational or irrational. Thaler comes close to thinking differently when he notes how businesses misunderstand perceptions of fairness at their peril, because they risk losing customers forever if they are seen to engage in price-gouging during times of trouble.[56]

From a non-economic point of view "irrational" loss-aversion and fairness quite rationally sustain relations with webs of things and people, and "irrational" sunk-cost thinking quite rationally engages in the work of individual or collective memory, identity, and mourning. The idea that economic rationality misunderstands and is potentially corrosive of fundamental relations with others and with oneself is very old. And this has been taken up in modern critiques of relations of domination that are said to be sustained by the supposed instrumentality of economic reason: in addition to the domination of employers over employed the domination of humans over nature, of colonizer over colonized, of men over women.

But recall that the allocative chooser isn't exactly instrumental. Their choice begins not from the end to be accomplished, but from the self (or firm or household) and its preferences and budgets. When properly rational, whether having needed nudging to get there or not, this agent is efficient, but not necessarily effective. Instead of a story about the role of economic rationality in domination, could one tell a story about the role of economic rationality in subordination? Recall Mankiw's fourth principle, his link between action and interaction: "People Respond to Incentives." He continues as follows: "An **incentive** is something that induces a person to act, such as the prospect of a punishment or reward. Because rational people make decisions by comparing costs and benefits, they respond to incentives." Mankiw quotes the self-styled market libertarian Steven Landsburg as saying that all of economics can be summed up by "'People respond to incentives. The rest is commentary.'"[57] Incentives, the prospects of reward and punishment, are used in management. For both Mankiw and for the behavioral economist authors of *Nudge*, the notable thing about economically rational or aspiring-to-be-rational choosers is that they are eminently manageable.

Politics, including political leadership, is, as Aristotle tells us, different from management, or from what he called economics. Informed by but departing from modern critiques of economic reason that wrongly label it emptily instrumental or amoral, I tell a different story. It is a story about a serious ethics and a serious politics that attempted to bridge

Aristotle's distinction, and its transformation into something else. It is a story about a discourse aimed at attacking lordship and dependency changing into a science of incentives. Much of this story maps the redefinition or erasure of the "political" in political economy.

3
Political Economy

To understand how political economy became economics – and how this transition refined and made foundational the meaning and place of economic rationality in the discipline – demands a fresh understanding of the project of political economy. A fresh understanding of political economy is made difficult by a common mistake in how we think about economics, both within and outside the discipline. The mistake is to distinguish the science entirely from politics and from ethics. Economics' disavowal of its own ethics and politics is facilitated through ritual gestures. "Positive" economics says it is not "normative," concerned with how things *should* be, but instead just describes how things are and how they work. Things are and things work a certain way despite, or even against, our best intentions.

In his bestselling textbook, Gregory Mankiw, like others, names the Scottish moral philosopher Adam Smith as a founder, and as founding an amoral and apolitical scientific discipline of self-interest and its outcomes. Mankiw quotes perhaps the most famous passage of Smith's *An Inquiry into the Nature and Causes of the Wealth of Nations* (1776), which advertises a happy unintended consequence: "'It is not from the benevolence of the butcher, the brewer, or the baker, that we expect our dinner, but from their regard to their own interest.'"[1] The best approach for Smith would seemingly insulate political economy from political and ethical direction through the "obvious and simple system of natural liberty" (*WN* IV.ix.51, 687). Smith's "system" looks to many of his modern readers like the economic rationality at the core of a value-free science at work, like the free allocative choosing of individuals producing micro and macro efficiencies assessed by a dispassionate student of social processes. But that is a misreading of Smith's aims and assumptions. Heterodox economists and historically oriented political theorists and moral philosophers carefully read Smith. They know there is much more to his political economy, that it is very much a politics and an ethics. They use Smith to "bring politics and morality back" into economics, in a new political economy, or a new emphasis on ethics, or other purported re-moralization or re-politicization of economic life. At their best, these projects remind us of the inseparability of economic and political life and moral life, even as they reinforce the false picture of a discipline supposed to have done away with ethics and politics in the twentieth century and beyond. At their worst these projects can reinforce the centrality of individual allocative choice at the heart of economics, as if what is called for is more ethical or more politically informed choices.

However, economics and economic rationality *are already* a politics and an ethics. They manage to do their politics and ethics, in part, by disavowing them. Both economists and their critics see the creature of economic rationality, the figure of rational allocative choice, as amoral and apolitical, and strictly instrumental. Yet economic rationality is not, as its defenders and many critics portray it, empty and instrumental. It is neither simply a heuristic assumption nor a neutral description; it is not amoral or apolitical. Economic rationality descends from a virtue well known to Smith and his contemporaries: from economy, or the careful administration of resources, which is recommended by the ancient virtue of prudence. And, wittingly or not, behavioral critics have lately brought economic rationality's political character out of hiding.

Recent skirmishes in the discipline between behavioralists and their targets highlight rationality's prescriptive character. They bring out the connection between choice and rule, the connection between choice and "making the right choices," and between choice and economic expertise, and expose how a choice explanation of political-economic failure, whether choice is figured as rational or irrational, serves, at least by omission, to politically legitimate the circumstances of failure. If, for example, "Greed and corruption helped to create" the global financial crisis of 2008, but "simple human frailty played a key role,"[2] then the crisis-generating problems are moral and cognitive, which calls for lessons in relevant virtues rather than a political analysis pressing for political change.

One common, and apparently more political, analysis of the crash was to attribute it to the institutional changes encouraged by the "deregulatory" model of Anglo-American capitalism promoted by influential neoliberal theorists like the University of Chicago's Milton Friedman. Within the profession, however, this could reduce to a conflict pitting empirical "truth" against mathematical "beauty." Mathematical economists were admonished that real markets, as opposed to the ones in their models, fail, and that they needed to work harder like their empirical colleagues to grasp the messiness of an economy that solicits but eludes representation.[3] Such rhetoric legitimates, for a range of economics-trained experts and the public at large, the idea that there is a discrete, machine-like reality named "the economy," and that scientists with proper methods are the ones to diagnose and fix it. Economists in the US Federal Reserve, and elsewhere, recommended unprecedented monetary and fiscal action in response to the crash of 2008 and the accelerating downturn of early 2020, suggesting not so much a new direction as that massive state action in support of collapsing markets is the neoliberalism of crisis. Technical or administrative fixes then supplement mental and moral fixes, all sidestepping directly political questions and answers (about justice, powerful interests, the purposes of government, etc.), beyond a narrow debate among disciplinary experts over proper policy.[4]

In other words, although oppositions between dominant postclassical tribes in economics are certainly important, their debates serve to reinforce what is common, if often only implicitly, between them: a conviction that *this* discipline has the supremely relevant political expertise. Economic expertise for the most part models behavior as choice, where its diverse recommendations for "policy choice" (again, whether considered "interventionist" or not) respond to and guide interactions among the choices of the governed. If allocative choice is the way of the world for a range of economics, a basic foundation of the positive science, the advantage of a glance at Friedman's popular work is that it embraces choice's normativity, and it shows, *pace* Friedman, the distance between the political theory of economics and that of Adam Smith.

With Rose Friedman, Friedman published *Free to Choose* in 1980, his sequel to 1962's *Capitalism and Freedom*. Friedman saw himself as reviving Smith, appealing to both freedom of choice and efficiency and showing the happy connection between them. More germane than Smith, although negatively, is the first book of Aristotle's *Politics* and its celebration of political space and political speech. Smith democratized Aristotle, embracing many more voices by adapting and rewriting Aristotle deep into society. With his "political oeconomy" he deliberately overran Aristotle's distinction between politics and economics (*oikonomia*). Friedman insists on a stark contrast à la Aristotle, while reversing the latter's valorization of politics over economics. Aristotle argued that politics is the realm of freedom, where one persuades and is persuaded by equals as to the justice or advantage of a common course of action; economics, by contrast, involves the management of subordinates. *Capitalism and Freedom* argues that politics is coercive and, by contrast, the economy coordinates freely, without coercion. For Friedman, the most tolerable politics is found in local government, but not because its smaller scale affords a more accessible platform for the exercise and development of political voice. Instead, local government operates like a seller in a market, because it must compete for residents with the power of exit.[5] "If I do not like what my local community does, be it in sewage disposal, or zoning, or schools, I can move to another local community and, although few may take this step, the mere possibility acts as a check."[6] Argument and persuasion have nothing to do with it, just as they don't really have anything to do with the choice-driven and choice-driving information/incentive/distribution machine that is Friedman's price system.[7]

In the later *Free to Choose*, Friedman is newly "influenced by a fresh approach to political science that has come mainly from economists." This approach

> treats the political system symmetrically with the economic system. Both are regarded as markets in which the outcome is determined by the interaction among persons pursuing their own self-interests (broadly interpreted) rather than by the social goals the participants find it advantageous to enunciate.[8]

"Pursuing self interest" here means choosing rationally in the textbook sense of economic rationality (which, as Friedman reminds us, isn't mere selfishness). Applied beyond economics narrowly understood, self-interest informs a new "political economy," in Mankiw's sense from his *Principles of Economics*.[9] Is this the interest from which I can expect Smith's baker to bake and part with his bread? Friedman thinks so – he gives full credit to Smith – but it isn't, really. Smith's interest is pointed to and assembled by way of conversation, perhaps less by the baker and more by the consumer, who appeals "not to [the butcher's or baker's] humanity but to their self-love" (*WN* I.ii.2, 27). Interest here is explicitly at least in part a relation, and thus more evidently *inter-est* than Friedman's interest, that is, something existing between, resonating the Latin etymology of the word. This difference in classical interest's situation makes a political, political-scientific, and ethical difference. It is in the microeconomic revision of classical interest that we can trace economics' transformation of the politics of political economy: its transformation in dominant hands into a thinly disguised science of self- and social management.

Friedman's reversal of Aristotle was aimed at expanding freedom understood as choice. "Free markets" enable and reflect choice; government "intervention" in markets restricts it. But economists opposed to Friedman's normative economics, for example the RAND corporation and Ivy League alumni who transformed US federal policymaking through the Kennedy and Johnson years,[10] interpreted individual interest and social alternatives in identical choice terms, even as they were more confident in the motives and capacities of what they took to be disinterested government officials, and more attuned to the failures of markets.

Smith's project, by contrast with postwar economics, was not about choice or the liberation of choice, but about dependence and the liberation from dependence. Many parents in our economic era have figured out that to get children to behave, simply let them choose from a menu of choices. Yet, governing in and through choice doesn't necessarily bear any relationship to developing independence, and may even run counter to it, thereby making childhood permanent. Smith's concern was to speed the reformation he saw taking place of a world where vast majorities suffered the status of children for their whole lives; vast majorities were dependent upon their superiors, whether or not dependence afforded them much choice, as it certainly might in some cases. In fact, one can think in ideal-typical terms of European feudalism as being a world of universal lordship and bondage: whether more or less free in Friedman's sense, everyone has a master, even the king, who has a master in God. With the decline of this world, needing cooperation of great multitudes with the rise of the division of labor doesn't, according to Smith, require dependence in this servile sense.[11]

The advance of impersonal dependence through commerce and the division of labor is, for Smith, consistent with spreading equality and freedom in personal independence. Smith's promotion of markets is about liberating voice as well as making provision for exit, and liberating voice beyond the men of property celebrated by early-modern republicans inspired by Aristotle, Cicero, and other classical sources. If republicans cried for liberty against domination by political tyrants and foreign conquerors, then Smith looked to what he saw as commerce's capacity to undermine this domination, as well as domination in the great households of some men of property themselves. Smith's text famously references a natural "propensity to truck, barter, and exchange" (*WN* I.ii.1, 25), but a close reading suggests that a concern with *truckling* animates his work. He thinks that too much of society, especially beyond Britain, speaks and acts in this fawning and servile, because dependent, way, which flows from existing modes of power and privilege. Truckling is perfectly self-interested, in the economists' sense, in the context of domination and personal dependence; it might even be a necessary survival strategy.

Jeremy Bentham, Smith's younger contemporary, doesn't get much recognition in histories of economics, at least not those penned in the twentieth century and beyond. His importance was, however, much better understood in the nineteenth century. Here is Alfred Marshall, certainly Britain's, and probably the world's, most prominent economist at the turn of the twentieth century:

> But on the whole the most influential of the immediate successors of Adam Smith [to the growth of economic science] was Bentham ... He was an uncompromising logician and an ardent reformer. He was an enemy of all artificial distinctions between different classes of men ...
>
> It was enough for [the disciples of Bentham] to discuss the tendencies of man's action on the supposition that everyone was always on the alert to find out what course would best promote his own interest, and was free and quick to follow it.[12]

In Bentham's own political economy, Smith's critique of the limits of state knowledge is systematized in the idea of the superiority of this interested alertness, a systematization usually credited to Friedrich Hayek's twentieth-century neoliberal economics.[13] More important to the development of economics than Bentham's political economy, though, was his general art and science of government and its understanding of *interest* as the foundation of a theory of motivation. Interest in Bentham's sense, as opposed to Smith's from the *Wealth of Nations*, is key to the ascendancy of microeconomic rational choice, to what Friedman thinks is just a common-sense understanding of self-interest.

Looking back on the nineteenth century Marshall's contemporary Beatrice Webb wrote:

> The Political Economy of Adam Smith was the scientific expression of the impassioned crusade of the 18th century against class tyranny and the oppression of the Many by the Few. By what silent transformation of events, by what unselfconscious transformation of

thought did it change itself into the 'Employers' Gospel' of the 19th century?[14]

As many besides Webb have noted, political economy after Smith has a counterrevolutionary cast. Several accounts argue persuasively that classical political economy presents a break with Smith's world.[15] Following the French Revolution a new social nature was declared, which was relatively independent of and superior to politics, most notoriously by Thomas Robert Malthus, the first British professor with "political economy" in his title. Scientific analysis of social nature invited the subsequent hardening of mutually constitutive race, class, and gender hierarchies intertwined with a new problematization of and preoccupation with sexuality,[16] well suited to increasingly aggressive and successful empire-building at home and abroad.

But political economy, while counterrevolutionary, was for the most part enlightened and progressive, and joined to and inspired by an explicitly political and moral project of sometimes radical democratic reform. It channeled Smith's project of independence into a zeal for universal, if strongly class-inflected, education in the virtue of economy. Political economy became an explicitly practical and utilitarian science, analogous to medicine. It studied the natural rhythms of the social body to develop an art of government to draw forth the social body's capacity to provide general prosperity and happiness.

Ironically, political economy lost the "political" and became economics when it adopted the idea of individual interest at the core of the most theoretically radical, conventionalist (but hardly conventional), and extensive of counterrevolutionary Enlightenment political projects: Jeremy Bentham's legislative science. The core of Bentham's art and science of government, as Marshall understood, was his theory of interest: Bentham boldly asserted the in-principle calculable commensurability of everything that might inform an individual's conduct. According to Bentham, then, everything I might do, and everything I expect to happen from doing it, can effectively be weighed in prospect against everything else I might do and what might follow from it. What allows for subjective commensurability in his scheme is expected pleasure and pain, whether my own direct pleasure or the pleasure I take from your pleasure because I'm sympathetic to you, and so on. It is Bentham's theory of interest, cut free of its own republican moorings, that inaugurates the economic rationality that powers much postclassical economic analysis. Thus a science born in the critique of domination, muted in mainstream voices until taken up with vigor by Bentham's protegé John Stuart Mill, can lose sight of its original target. It can even, as Webb suggests, perform the opposite function of giving succor to a new class of overlords. Economics does such palliative work when as a moral science it retreats to the agent, obscures class, and leaves the problem of domination behind, proceeding instead exclusively from the philosophically idiosyncratic and politically transformative idea of reason as a matter of allocative choice.[17]

Reading Adam Smith

Bentham was a fierce, lifelong critic of the English common-law system. One of his complaints was the customary and unthought-out punishment of what he took to be victimless crimes. In *Defence of Usury* (1787) Bentham took Adam Smith to task for inconsistency: although Smith argued against many other prohibitions on freedom of commerce, he supported anti-usury legislation: restrictions on agreements between lenders and borrowers above a stipulated rate of interest. *Defence of Usury* begins as follows:

> Among the various species of or modifications of liberty, of which on different occasions we have heard so much in England, I do not recollect ever seeing any thing yet offered in behalf of the liberty of making one's own terms in money-bargains. From so general and universal neglect ... this meek and unassuming species of liberty has been suffering much injustice.[18]

The passage pokes fun at much louder liberty-talk – the natural-rights radical Whig discourses that had inspired American independence – and alludes to Smith's *Wealth of Nations*, in particular the early chapter on "the Principle which gives occasion to the Division of Labour." For Smith, what gives occasion to the division of labor, the very engine of the wealth of the nations, is free exchange. Strange as it may seem to our ears, Smith's liberty to truck and barter, to settle one's own terms in bargains, is not about *choice*, thus not about "self-interest" in Friedman's modern sense. Instead it is about freedom of encounter and discussion – about equality. It is about the stuff of politics, or at least it quite consciously and deliberately lifts the classical description of politics from Aristotle, which is defined in opposition to *oikonomia* or household rule, and shows it at work beyond narrowly political relations.[19] This in turn opens the benefits of classical politics – its freedom, equality of standing, and creative uses of speech – beyond the limited class of free householders recognized in civic humanist and republican letters.

Smith's first use of the word "bargain" in *Wealth of Nations* is in this second chapter: "Whoever offers to another a bargain of any kind, proposes to do this. Give me that which I want, and you shall have this which you want …" The sentences precede the often-cited first textual use of "interest" in the singular as a noun, "It is not from the benevolence of the butcher … but from their regard to their own interest." Smith labels the bargain as "talk" (*WN* I.ii.2, 26–27).[20] Aristotle wrote, "language serves to declare what is advantageous and what is the reverse, and…therefore… what is just and what is unjust."[21] As Smith put it in lectures preceding *Wealth of Nations*, even a simple purchase is rhetorical: "The offering of a shilling, which to us appears to have so plain and simple a meaning, is in reality offering an argument to persuade one to do so and so as it is for his interest."[22] In chapter two Smith next introduces the beggar, who is exceptional because he, by contrast, "chuses" (this is the first use in the text of any variant of "choice") to depend on the benevolence of others. Yet even though the beggar's money comes from an occupation viewed as abject and servile, Smith notes he purchases his dinner with his alms, on a footing at that point of free equality with any other buyer or seller (*WN* I.ii.2, 27). Just as genuinely political association à la Aristotle is a mode where one's words, no matter what one's specific virtues, wealth, or family background, can claim equality with those of others, Smith says this is true of the modal scene of exchange.

Smith's emphasis on argument and persuasion, his insistence that the place of exchange is one of freedom, equality, and absence of domination (what Karl Marx a century later would lampoon as "a very Eden of the innate rights of man")[23] aims to resonate with readers' civic humanist intuitions built from centuries of uptake of especially Aristotle and Cicero.[24] Smith consciously locates virtues associated with the *polis* or *res publica* in the common life of society, just as he had located moral virtues associated with Church and hearth in common life in *The Theory of Moral Sentiments* (1759). For Aristotle, politics uses and enhances our distinctively human capacity for speech. Again, the *polis* is a realm of freedom where citizens meet as equals to persuade one another of the justice or advantage of a course of cooperation. It contrasts with the household, or *oikos*, a realm of necessity marked by inequality in which persuasion plays less of a role than command (and thus coercion).

Political economy would have been an oxymoron for Aristotle.[25] The phrase suggests, in its root sense, managing the commonwealth as a giant household,[26] which Aristotle associated with "barbarian" despotism. Smith is a critic of large households (while praising small ones), seeing the households of the great as despotic places breeding servility. The politics and ethics of servility are a major concern for Smith. Servility is destructive, equal independence is constructive. His sly rewriting of Aristotle's *Politics* into the life of society is couched in a broader critique of Aristotle and Cicero and their worlds; Smith sees classical republican freedom as dependent upon slavery, and rejects its aristocratic basis. He promotes shopkeepers and artisans and even petty peddlers and laborers to a kind of democratic standing in the realm of exchange, which, according to him, is the driver of the division of labor and thus general enrichment in every sense. He sees the expansion of this realm, the expansion of commerce, as a major cause of the destruction of a despised feudal order of great households.

The other side of servility resulting from dependence is domination, which substitutes command for persuasion. "The pride of man makes him love to domineer, and nothing mortifies him so much as to be obliged to condescend to persuade his inferiors ... (H)e will generally prefer the service of slaves to that of freemen" (*WN* III.ii, 388). Smith in chapter two describes this relationship of domination and subordination as one shared by other animals, animals who like Aristotle's are incapable of genuine cooperation, that is, cooperation from persuasion. "A puppy fawns upon its dam ... Man sometimes uses the same arts with his brethren, and when he has no other means ... endeavours by every servile and fawning attention to obtain their good will" (*WN* I.ii.2, 26). Just as it applies to a noble household this might describe how the beggar proceeds, when he chooses to rely on others' benevolence.

The voice of Aristotle's *zoon politikon* is using speech: according to him humans show themselves to be distinctively political animals through conversation. Likewise for Smith, other animals might appear to act in concert, and they use "gestures and natural cries," but their apparent cooperation is instead "the accidental concurrence of their passions in the same object at that particular time. Nobody ever saw a dog make a fair and deliberate exchange of one bone for another with another dog" (*WN* I.ii.2, 25–26). As his early lecture version puts it, hounds chasing a hare are "helpfull to each other and divide the labour, but this does not arise from any contract ... they generally quarrell about her after she is killed" (*LJ* (A) vi.44, 347).[27] Striking a bargain, as Francis Bacon had suggested, uses language and avoids violence: "The second blow makes the fray, The second word makes the bargaine."[28] Commerce contrasts not only with the hierarchy of feudal domination, it contrasts with the conquest and war so prevalent among the ancients.[29] Smith's dogs can't coordinate their practice in this way, but humans can. The dogs could be independently and mutely and even rationally *choosing* to work together, but they aren't really cooperating.

Smith's creative transposition of Aristotle begs a question: what about the possibilities of cooperation among equals afforded by politics itself? Smith's neoliberal admirers are correct that he is suspicious of politics. His suspicion flows from analysis of a mode of free egalitarian cooperation different from exchange, though not in Smith's work ever neatly and analytically distinguished from it: "People of the same trade seldom meet together, even for merriment and diversion, but the conversation ends in a conspiracy against the publick, or in some contrivance to raise prices" (*WN* I.x.c.27, 145). The whole story of the "policy of Europe" mandating liberty-restricting apprenticeships and otherwise regulating the individual trades, not to mention the licenses granted to the chartered monopolies of the British empire and all the commercial restrictions they entailed, were for Smith manifestations of this nefarious cooperation. There is no way "consistent with liberty and justice" to prevent this from happening. Smith accepts combinations as a given; there is no sense that markets do or could ever somehow operate completely free of such political-economic arrangements, much less the legal and moral frameworks in which they are embedded. What is key is to, as far as possible, withdraw the legal supports and especially the legal ratifications of, and mandates for, these conspiracies of the trades.

To a modern political economist in the Mankiw textbook mold, Smith's problem looks familiar: monopoly "rent-seeking" by economic actors that can, for example, produce protectionist legislation. But the modern model misunderstands Smith's political concerns, and how political aims are embedded into almost every aspect of what we call his economics. The new political economy is simply the extension of an ostensibly depoliticized economics beyond market-priced goods and services and into a formally political domain. Smith's project counters domination, and the new political economy has no understanding of domination, just a concern about the restriction of choice and the raising of prices.[30] Smith promotes a mode of cooperation, that is, market exchange, that he is confident relies on independence and erodes dependence. The idea for Smith is to facilitate the building of spaces of equal encounter. For him it is unthinkable that one could do this without understanding the virtues sustaining, and sustained by, equal encounter, virtues absent from later economic modeling. For Smith, recognizing and expanding equal encounter also requires an awareness and analysis of class society, an awareness retained by classical political economy but assumed away by modern economics.

Smith doesn't solve the problems of freedom and domination he raises, but he does point to their complexities. His concern throughout is not whether lordship is "private" or "public" in our terms; those terms are wrongly projected onto Smith's whole discussion of what Friedman and others would call coercion, as somehow following from his suspicion of modes of state action. Smith cares instead whether lordship is lordship, whether domination is able to persist or will give way to independence. Indeed, "All for ourselves, and nothing for other people, seems, in every age of the world, to have been the vile maxim of the masters of mankind" (*WN* III.iv.10, 418). This passage appears in a discussion of how commerce undermined feudal masters: the heads of great households diverted their resources to consumption, and thereby inadvertently loosened their hold on servants converted into independent producers of luxury goods. The slow workings of childish avarice in one class of people and of self-bettering industry in the other secured a political and social revolution "of the greatest importance to the publick happiness" (*WN* III.iv, 422). To reduce these dynamics to the simple operation of self-interest in our terms misses the whole quietly polemical, and thoroughly political, thrust of the account.

Smith connects this commercial revolution to the more narrowly political revolution of the rise of monarchs and the decline of barons, and praises the relatively stable and mild laws of his time and place over the despotism prevalent in parts of continental Europe and beyond. There are contradictions and countertendencies here. Smith, like much of political economy after him, is pro-settler colonialist and anti-imperialist.[31] American colonies, in particular British North America, are places in which, because of an abundance of supposedly available land, wages can rise quickly. Prosperity can rapidly develop with benefits widely shared. Unlike many others, Smith laments the injustice done to indigenous peoples (see e.g. *WN* IV.i.32, 448), but there is generally not much regard paid to their interests and to indigenous agricultural and political practices in his work. Smith's scattered remarks on "savages" are much more layered and complex than those of his nineteenth-century successors, even as they serve settler-colonial myths. His portraits included a noble-savage projection imagining indigenous Americans as near-superhuman Stoics, an economic everyman image of them as primitive rational barterers, a conjectural history of development understanding them as poor and scattered non-cultivators, and, most interesting of all, a related progressive-regressive understanding implying that European modernity is bad for women's power: "In North America, the woemen are consulted concerning the carrying on of war, and in every important undertaking. The respect paid to woemen in modern times is very small" (*LJ* II.105, 439). (This last begs the question of how commerce and the division of labor bring about independence if they have produced a condition of servitude for half the population.) The work on colonies is anti-imperialist in lamenting the oppression of metro-politan domination, as part of Smith's more general critique of misguided mercantilist policies. The gift of comparatively mild and regular government allowed the British North American colonies to thrive. Yet one significant downside of freer government (in comparison to the more arbitrary government of French colonies) is that it protects and even nurtures a particularly egregious form of domination, by giving reliable recognition to slaveholders' property claims in the enslaved (*WN* IV.vii.b.54, 587; *LJ* iii.110–111, 185).

Wealth of Nations is animated by a concern for liberty understood as independence and non-domination, domination that can and does occur in the "private" sphere, not only outside of it.[32] It is curious how little Smith writes about politics narrowly speaking. Scholars speculate that he had his long-planned and still unfinished book on jurisprudence burned at his death so as not to compromise the growing success of his other work. He was bolder when it came to the Church, making arguments favorable to disestablishment and the plurality of sects (e.g. *WN* V.i.g.8, 792–793). The "weak state" and "weak church" of his contemporary Scotland[33] were, Smith thought, favorable to the bustling invention he admired in the many small manufactories he visited. We don't know much about Smith's politics, but we have a number of clues. Clearly, non-arbitrary rule of independent men by what John Locke had called "settled laws" is preferred. It might not matter so much who makes and impartially enforces these laws, in which case politics narrowly understood can be downplayed.[34] Here again, however, there is some ambivalence.

Even Smith's ethics, and his psychology, have a deeply political aspect. The problem of classical liberty is a problem, in part, of standing. Writing in a profoundly hierarchical society, Smith's egalitarian orientation is on display in his ethics, for example in his qualified elevation of self-interest. He recognizes what others saw as the baseness of the self-interest of the petty tradesman as an assemblage of at least minor virtues. Smith's teacher Francis Hutcheson was an early advocate of the view that morality came naturally to humans, but Hutcheson's focus on benevolence made it seem as if benevolence laid exclusive claim to the moral life. And some people are much better positioned to afford benevolence than others. Smith had a more expansive and plural view of ethical behavior and its sources. "Sympathy," what we call empathy, was at its heart,[35] and respect for the rules of justice was non-negotiable, but Smith embeds these in a larger framework that looks favorably, albeit in a qualified way, on a range of classical perspectives elevating propriety and self-command. Writing about Hutcheson and his hostility to self-love Smith stresses that "Regard to our own private happiness and interest ... appear upon many occasions ... very praise-worthy qualities ..." Meanwhile, "Carelessness and want of oeconomy are universally disapproved of ... as proceeding ... from a want of the proper attention to the objects of self-interest" (*TMS* VII.ii.3.16, 304). Smith appreciates the foresight and forbearance that ancient traditions of prudence the world over recognize and promote (as seen, for example, in Confucius' *Analects*).

"Oeconomy" in this sense is not mere ordering or arrangement. It is such administration with an eye to reducing waste, that is, efficiency. Fighting waste would go on to be the signal explicit or implicit virtue of classical and modern political economy and economics. Economy is key to modern economic rationality, to the rationality of allocative choice. Smith's appreciation of what goes into self-interest doesn't extend, however, to lifting economy and allied practices above other concerns. Economy is praiseworthy in exhibiting the virtue of prudence, and good economy may be a necessary condition for the exercise of other virtues such as liberality, or generosity. But the moral systems coming closest to the modern rationality assumed in economic modeling and prescribed by behavioral economists, what Smith calls "those Systems which make Virtue consist in Prudence" (*TMS* VII. ii.2, 294), are "altogether inconsistent" with his own (*TMS* VII.ii.2.13, 298). This is not because they are confused with simple selfishness, but because they are reductionist, and because they don't understand the primacy of *relations*, especially with others but, by extension, with oneself. They exhibit "the propensity to account for all appearances from as few principles as possible" (*TMS* VII.ii.2.14, 299), and they can't ultimately account for one's need to be respected and loved as ends in themselves.

Smith doesn't think a lot of economy by itself, especially when exercised at the expense of other virtues. "To be anxious, or to be laying a plot either to gain or to save a single shilling, would degrade the most vulgar tradesman in the opinion of all his neighbours" (*TMS* III.6.6, 173). Even a less base and more comprehensive rule-following prudence, if it is directed only at one's own affairs, merely "commands a certain cold esteem" (*TMS* VI.i.14, 216). Smith does, however, much admire a superior prudence, what one might call political prudence, far removed from simple self-interest or simple benevolence, however understood.

> We talk of the prudence of the great general, of the great statesman, of the great legislator. Prudence is, in all these cases, combined with many greater and more splendid virtues; with valour, with extensive and strong benevolence, with a sacred regard to the rules of justice, and all these supported by a proper degree of self-command. This superior prudence ... is the best head joined to the best heart. (*TMS* VI.i.15, 216)

Smith's project is a liberal one: it significantly adapts and adjusts a republican worldview to fully embrace an emerging commercial world.[36] But the republican worldview remains, and even at times predominates. However much he elevates the humble workings of social life it is *public* life, properly lived, that is here exciting Smith's greatest admiration. Unlike many of his neoliberal admirers and their critics Smith clearly takes as a given a *res publica*: an appropriate and supremely important field of exercise for the judgment and action of this superior prudence.

Smith added the above quotation as part of revisions for the 1790 edition of *The Theory of Moral Sentiments*. This was the year he died, not long after the storming of the Bastille in Paris in 1789, which heralded for many fellow Enlightenment writers the advent of a new political universe. In *Wealth of Nations* Smith looked some to the future of commerce, not only the past and present. What he saw there was not all good. He worried about the effects on workers of the increasing division of labor; this informed his proposals for universal education. He noted struggles between workers and employers over wages, and lamented how practice and law favored employer combinations to lower them and disfavored worker combinations to raise them. Emma Rothschild describes how both sides of a debate over establishment of a minimum wage used Smith's arguments after his death.[37] Perhaps the question for Smith in this situation, as in any number of others, would be, "what does superior prudence prescribe?" Rothschild persuasively argues that minimum wage advocates were truer to Smith, even as the fight was lost for a century and more. She and others note how many of Smith's students and associates, most prominently Dugald Stewart, were anxious to rescue the master from the taint of political radicalism in the midst of Britain's fears over contagion from, and war with, revolutionary France. The effort did a lot to shape the new science of political economy, revering Smith as a founder. Political economy domesticated and transformed, even as it took up, powerful strains of Smith's politics and ethics (some escaped into popular political economy including socialist political economy). Fighting dependence and domination would, however, still be the broader project for John Stuart Mill, the most prominent of late-stage classical political economists, writing in the middle of the nineteenth century. But the most fateful trend for the story of economic rationality was economics' gradual suppression of a worldly field of often clashing interests, settling on an encompassing subjective theory of individual interest that elevated economy over other concerns. Once agency was fully rewritten as allocative choice, domination in

Smith's sense would no longer remain a coherent idea, much less a concern.

From Malthus to Mill

Smith's worry about the reductionism and explanatory limits of "systems which make virtue consist in prudence" would prove prophetic for political economy and economics. Yet he lacked Bentham's sense of the governmental power and creative potential of such a system. Well understood and well deployed, the political economists generally thought it could help make their world more Smithian: freer, more egalitarian, richer, and happier. Besides, "the propensity to account for all appearances from as few principles as possible" is the mark of good science. In the eighteenth century it was already contributing to the great successes of natural philosophy's apparent ability to unlock the secrets of nature. Science and government came together in the political earthquake of the French Revolution. It suddenly appeared possible, to enthusiastic supporters, for people to seize power and govern themselves transparently on scientific grounds. The revolution seemed to confirm that forms of inquiry manifesting in technical improvements could similarly lead to social and political improvements, pointing to an infinite horizon of progress in human affairs.

It's easy to forget the connections between classical political economy and political radicalism because of the ferocity of some of the former's nineteenth-century critics and because of the fallout from the French Revolution, especially in Britain. Also, the American and French revolutions were animated by natural-rights discourses that were in significant tension with the conventionalism about property and other developed institutions informing Smith and later political economy: much republican rhetoric had a backward-looking quality. But, in conservative Britain at least, it was not at all clear that Smith's support for a "system of natural liberty" could be separated from other calls for liberty.[38] New associations like the London Corresponding Society sprang up, ratifying the establishment's fear of revolutionary contagion. Although no revolutionary, in his opposition to "tumult," William

Godwin was a forward-looking visionary, like the more commerce-friendly Marquis de Condorcet in France. His 1793 *Political Justice*, like Thomas Paine's 1792 *Rights of Man*, was read aloud in popular gatherings. Godwin indicted all institutions, such as law, property, marriage, and so on, as corrupting and enslaving, and predicted that they would fall away in the face of substantial improvements in knowledge and the education of individual judgment.[39]

Political economy's notorious nineteenth-century reputation as the "Employers' Gospel," hated alike by nostalgic conservatives, nostalgic radicals, humanitarians of various stripes, and future-oriented revolutionaries, can seem reasonable given Robert Malthus. Malthus, scathingly described as qualified "for the delicate office of conscience-keeper to the rich and great,"[40] made his reputation with a second, greatly expanded edition of *An Essay on the Principle of Population* (1803). The first, anonymous, edition of *Population* (1798) was a more narrow and fatalistic work aimed directly at Godwin and Condorcet (both named in the subtitle), and the idea of unbounded human improvement. But some of the more fundamental changes to the 1803 edition Malthus had made in dialogue with Godwin, who received Malthus's criticisms quite positively.[41] The most important of Malthus's changes demonstrate that the new science of political economy, despite its subsequent reputation, carried forward much of the emancipatory vision of Godwin, though in less of a hurry. Malthus's 1798 *Population* had argued that different rates of agricultural and population growth insured that improvement would always in turn produce crisis, guaranteeing a perpetual oscillation in the human condition between temporary prosperity and more lasting misery. Now, under pressure from Anglican orthodoxy,[42] in dialogue with Godwin, and having more carefully compared Britain with other countries, Malthus saw a way forward. The title of the new work is explicitly utilitarian: *An Essay on the Principle of Population; or, a view of its past and present effects on human happiness; with an enquiry into our prospects respecting the future removal or mitigation of the evils which it occasions.*[43] Reformed English institutions and the education of the poor in "moral restraint," including delaying marriage until children could be supported, could break the cycle of prosperity and misery and produce permanent progress. Prudence would save the day.

"Savages" lacked prudence. Development out of this parlous state was about an exchange with non-human nature demanding increased reason, reason defined as calculating foresight in the service of economy. The crucial institution savages lacked, according to Malthus and like-minded contemporaries, was property, which provides the security foresight relies upon for its proper exercise. Yet they saw many of the English poor, in particular the dependent poor who relied upon the despised Poor Laws, as themselves wretched. The nineteenth-century trope opposing "virtuous" Scots and "feckless" Irishmen brought urgency to the need to help the English poor by removing perverse incentives and educating them in economy, to contribute to their independence and incrementally better their condition.

Thus classical political economy was thickly institutional because "civilizational" in comparison to later economics (and even through the marginal turn, as seen in the work of Marshall). Especially in its popular mainstream forms, it could be explicit about the secular evangelism that is quietly evident in the new behavioral economics, working as it did within natural limits in order to help its subjects better exercise the virtue of economy. Jane Marcet was host to Malthus, to David Ricardo – Malthus's friend and intellectual sparring partner – and to James Mill, the muse to Ricardo's monumental *Principles of Political Economy and Taxation* (1817), housemate of Bentham, and father of John Stuart. Marcet wrote the anonymous bestselling *Conversations on Political Economy* (first published 1816), which went through at least fourteen editions, was translated into several languages, and was more widely read than the works of Malthus, Ricardo, and Jean-Baptiste Say, from which it drew. In Marcet's work, according to Say, "the soundest principles are explained in a familiar and pleasing style,"[44] and Say in turn borrowed from Marcet.

The *Conversations*, a dialogue between a teacher, Mrs. B, and a precocious student, Caroline, displays a dominant understanding of civilization as the development of a kind of social nature; it demonstrates the role of political economy as an explicitly utilitarian practical science, like medicine, that can understand and aid in this development. Mrs. B defines the new science: "Political economy treats of the formation, the distribution, and the consumption of wealth; it teaches us the causes which promote or prevent its increase, and their influence on the happiness or misery of society" (*CPE*, 18). Political economy consists of both "theory and practice; the science and the art." The art, which "relates ... to legislation ... consists in doing whatever is requisite to contribute to the increase of national wealth, and avoiding whatever would be prejudicial to it." The problem is that "governments ... have frequently arrested the natural progress of wealth when it was in their power to have accelerated it" (*CPE*, 21). Crucial to this "natural progress" is security from an explicitly conventional institution implemented by art, that is, property. In response to Caroline's view that virtue and happiness are more important than wealth Mrs. B assures her that the principles of political economy "all tend to promote the happiness of nations, and of the purest morality." The science "tends to moderate all unjustifiable ambition, by showing that the surest means of increasing national prosperity are peace, security, and justice." Confusion is cleared up by the first lesson: wealth isn't about individuals, or about money or some other narrow idea of riches, but about the social accumulation of exchangeable things of utility. If we focus on the many and not just on their ruling classes we recognize this is at least a necessary, if not sufficient, condition for general happiness (*CPE*, 22–29).

The book rigorously engages a comprehensive list of the main topics of classical political economy in detail, including capital, wages and population, rent, interest, value, money, and foreign trade. Although of a notably conservative cast – one of its aims clearly is to "reconcile" its reader "to the inequality of the distribution of wealth," and to assure of a harmony of interest between rich and poor[45] – its stress throughout is on the gradual progress of all classes. As with Malthus, the poor especially require discipline to avoid excess reproduction if they are to have any hope of independence. A "healthy and hard-working man may, if he be economical, almost always lay aside something as the beginning of a little capital, which by additional savings accumulates"

(*CPE*, 101). Such accumulation by a worker brings "a little independence for himself and his family" (*CPE*, 182). But political economy targets more than the majority poor for reform. Marcet's volume concludes with a discussion of consumption, or "expenditure," addressing the vexed subject of luxury and disciplining the rich. Caroline had earlier hoped to abolish rents because landlords, "these wealthy men, who indulge in ease and repose, are no better members of society than the indolent savage" (*CPE*, 229). Even as Mrs. B cites Bentham approvingly in defense of luxury, it remains true that "illiberal parsimony and extravagant prodigality [are] extremes to be avoided." Yet "there are so many gradations in the scale between them, that every man must draw the line for himself, according to the dictates of his good sense and his conscience ..." On the one hand, liberal expenditure by the rich benefits everyone, as it provides for the work and development of the poor. On the other hand, any outright waste by the rich is "so much taken from that fund which provides maintenance and employment for the poor" (*CPE*, 478–480). Political economy's opponents across the spectrum saw it as undermining virtue, with its justification of the passion for gain and its critique of unintended consequences of charity, whether public, in the form of the Poor Laws, or private, in the form of alms for beggars. But political economy itself was a lesson in virtue for all classes: a lesson in economy, and in the independence and self-command that were said to be its virtuous cause and effect.

Say and Ricardo in their political economy were more intent to steer clear of moral controversy, but a variant of Marcet's disciplinary and progressive ethics and politics is evident in each. Say's *Traité d'économie politique* (1803) had specified politics and political economy as two different things: political economy is a science of wealth that any kind of regime, through proper administration, can use to bring prosperity. "If political liberty is more favourable to the development of wealth, it is indirectly, in the same manner that it is more favourable to general education."[46] But Say, like Malthus and Marcet, tied lasting prosperity to improvement, and both to happiness. Political economy advanced a theory of progress and the kind of rational administration needed for it, even as fears about natural limits increased, especially in English political economy. Despite the declared political neutrality of his science, Say was a confirmed republican, and in his French context "political economy was intended for the inculcation of virtue in a society of atheists."[47] Ricardo, a successful London stockbroker, engaged in debate with both Say and Malthus. Lines of argument elaborated in the *Principles* were offered in his 1815 essay disputing Malthus's argument for the Corn Laws' restriction of grain imports. Ricardo's suspicion of the aristocracy, and that his friend was being seduced by their arguments, comes through in the text. "It follows, then [from an analysis of the relationship between rent and profit], that the interest of the landlord is always opposed to the interest of every other class in the community." He concludes on a somewhat polemical note: "I shall greatly regret that considerations for any particular class are allowed to check the progress of the wealth and population of the country." If cheap imported food is a problem, why not, according to the same flawed logic, restrict agricultural improvements, which after all also lower rents?[48]

The politics of the *Principles of Political Economy and Taxation* are more subtle. The book is credited by later economists with introducing scientific modeling to the discipline, but the class analysis is largely unchanged, and Marcet's virtues do play a key role in progress. Following Malthus, Ricardo argues that the Poor Laws devalue the "prudence" critical for the poor to control their numbers and develop "independence."[49] For Ricardo, as for his contemporaries (all in this and other respects following Smith), the formation of capital itself is a function of the "parsimony" of the capitalist. (Nassau Senior, appointed to the first professorship in Britain exclusively for political economy, went so far as to substitute "the term Abstinence for that of Capital.")[50] And Ricardo, at the urging of James Mill, entered Parliament as an independent and reliably radical vote for free trade and political reform.

In classical political economy proper, economic rationality consolidates as a broadly utilitarian ideal: the science promotes economy, or rational administration to advance wealth, in the conduct of personal and state affairs. It might seem in the emerging quasi-consensus that Smith's ambiguous politics were now much less so: the lines between politics and society are well drawn, collective action is discouraged, and individual bettering of one's condition through economy encouraged. Yet the association between embracing political economy and fighting domination and dependence, though shrouded in some hands, remained strong. Consider the "tailor of Charing Cross," Francis Place. Place was a genuine bridge between working and middle-class radicals. He was a central figure in both the London Corresponding Society and the Chartist movement of the 1840s. In between, he was a patient organizer, voracious reader, and good friend and sometime housemate of Bentham and the elder Mill. Place rejected natural rights,[51] embraced Malthusian and Ricardian science, and his very biography shows the connection between political economy and political radicalism. His book on population laments Malthus's disposal to "favour the prejudices of the rich" and says of the poor that they know "that the whole practice of government, in respect to them, has been, and still is, an attempt to keep down the wages of labour ..." The poor know about the rich "that it has been the intention of ... them to reduce them to the most abject state of dependence" and that "while they are preached to, as it were, with one hand they are scourged with the other." Betterment of the condition of workers demanded repeal of the Combination Acts against unionization, which Place successfully agitated against. "No good reason has been or can be given for restraining the workmen and their employers from making their bargains in their own way, as other bargains are made." He advocates in the same breath free emigration, free trade, and collective bargaining, in a book notoriously calling for contraceptive knowledge as not only consistent with, but supportive of virtue.[52]

Place was an important influence for the young John Stuart Mill, which shows in the latter's anonymous advocacy of contraception in the radical *Black Dwarf*.[53] The relationship between sound political economy, the education of virtue, and accumulating social progress is nowhere clearer than in the younger Mill's monumental *Principles of Political Economy* (first edition 1848).[54] In the earlier "On the Definition of Political Economy" Mill had rigorously posited economic rationality at the core of the young science.

Political economy forwards "a definition of man, as a being who invariably does that by which he may obtain the greatest amount of necessaries, conveniences, and luxuries, with the smallest quantity of labour and physical self-denial with which they can be obtained in the existing state of knowledge."[55] A Catholic critic would, decades later, label this idea of human nature as maximization under constraint "*Homo economicus*," in one of the first uses of the phrase, writing of it (as critics do today) as an unrealistic account of human behavior.[56] Such criticism then and now ignores explicit acknowledgment of the definition's lack of realism. Abstraction is precisely the point in the development of the sciences, and "There is, perhaps, no action of a man's life in which he is neither under the immediate nor under the remote influence of any impulse but the mere desire of wealth" (*DPE*, 322). Here, and in *Principles*, the science of political economy is the study strictly of what Mill sees as "economical" activity, that is, activity concerned with the production and distribution of wealth. Political economy includes, however, consideration of two "perpetual antagonists" to the pursuit of wealth that "accompany it always as a drag, or impediment, and are therefore inseparably mixed up in the consideration of it." The drag comes from "aversion to labour" and "desire of the present enjoyment of costly indulgences" (*DPE*, 321–322).

Figuring out how to do more with less, then, requires embracing the very costs we are trying to reduce, that is, labor and self-denial. Political economy is thus the study of "economical" activity in another sense, which is all over Mill's *Principles*: economical activity as engendered by and producing economy. For example, competition produces economy: the market mechanism favors more economical producers, who can offer lower prices to economical consumers. "Providence," or foresight, and self-command, the virtues underpinning economy, are crucial to seeing and taking advantage of market opportunities as producer or consumer. When it comes to work and enjoyment, knowledge and timing are everything. Pleasure forgone now often produces more later.[57] Malthus's principle of population is a core illustration of the benefits and costs of restraint or its absence; education in and respect for it is critical to ameliorating the domination of women, and to the future of the working class as a whole.

English political economy had generally asserted a harmony of interests between employers and employed. Ricardo was of this view, but rapid industrialization was producing doubts for him by the time of the third edition of his *Principles*: workers were right in many circumstances to think of automation as a threat to their interests,[58] and this only contributed to socialist appropriations of Ricardian science. By the time of Mill's writing, much had changed from Smith's era. The machine was triumphant, the competitive superiority of large enterprises clear, and the artisan-era link between labor and reward, the whole basis of the "economical principle," the fundamental rationale underpinning both the justice and efficiency of liberal political economy, evidently broken by the wage system. The year 1848 was one of revolution on the Continent, pushing Mill to read extensively in socialist literature for a significant early revision of his *Principles*. Regarding the charge that communists have no incentive to work, Mill writes: "If Communistic labour might be less vigorous than that of a peasant proprietor, or a workman labouring on his own account, it would probably be more energetic than that of a labourer for hire, who has no personal interest in the matter at all" (*PPE*, 204–205). Mill finds that the model he favors, small proprietorship, is increasingly obsolete. *On Liberty* (1859) famously defined utility in terms of the "permanent interests of man as a progressive being."[59] For Mill these interests pointed to a gradual transition toward socialism: in his vision free trade among efficient worker cooperatives. He steered a course between conservatives and less "advanced" liberals defending property on the one side, and revolutionary or statist socialists and communists on the other.[60]

James Mill's essay on government for the *Encyclopedia Britannica* had argued for radical political reform on a Benthamic basis: it was the only way to promote the aggregate interests of the governed. Representative democracy is not about self-rule for its own sake, but allows individuals to make sure their interests, and not those of others, are served in politics. Fellow Benthamite radicals William Thompson and Anna Wheeler attacked the senior Mill's non-enfranchisement of women for entrenching servitude to fathers and husbands, and further suggested that the competitive system itself was counter to women's interests because of the isolated dependence on husbands engendered by childbirth and childcare. Only mutual interdependence in socialist cooperatives could promote full liberation.[61] In the hands of these and other theorists, and eventually the younger Mill himself, the republican push for non-domination, generally shared by classical political economy, demanded far-reaching, if still gradual, political-economic transformation. Perhaps the only way to meet the demands of interest was through cooperative association, which required a broad and deep education of character in a higher prudence beyond individual economy, so that one could see how firmly one's individual betterment was tied to collective goals. Many early socialists thought that the cooperative principle would effectively exploit the dynamics of esteem that Adam Smith had analyzed as crucial to the development and workings of individual prudence. Like Smith, they were concerned with addressing relations of domination. But many extended his struggle for equal standing beyond his exclusions, and all saw a need for a new dispensation in light of the interim emergence of industrial capitalism.

On interest: Back to Bentham

From Smith's butcher and baker forward, we think of interest, especially self-interest, as economic; but interest's configurations of rationality are inescapably political and moral. Albert Hirschman's *The Passions and the Interests* tracked the moral character of interest discourse in early-modern European letters. Interests here are "countervailing passions." Early introspective models deploy some passions, like desire for gain, to moderate others, like love of ease or desire for revenge. Reason alone is weak, but the interested self allies reason to the power of select passions to achieve discipline.[62] This is the comparatively predictable discipline of self-interest emphasized in classical political economy's promotion of the virtue of economy.

Interest is political, and not only in the aims of moralists to substitute constructive discipline for destructive passion, to make politics less about all-or-nothing aims and more about severable and negotiable parts. Interest-talk also descends from juridical and reason-of-state traditions pointing in two directions. One is toward a common object of concern shared with some in opposition to others, whether in foreign or domestic relations, giving us a rational way to sort allies from opponents. (When classical political economists write of a harmony or disharmony of interests they are using it in this way.) Another direction is toward a public interest binding political community through the articulation of what is needed or wanted and useful to all members, or conversely points to the common threat of its absence. (This is classical political economy's understanding of wealth, and perhaps more fundamentally of security.)

J. S. Mill criticized the "interest philosophy" of both his father and Bentham as crudely deductive and inadequate to the science of the social that the younger Mill thought necessary to an adequate art of government.[63] His most fundamental objection to Bentham was the latter's lack of concern with *character*.[64] This, argued Mill, was a scientific, moral and aesthetic, and political mistake. It was a scientific mistake because people's individual or national characters shaped their conduct, whereas Bentham emphasized simple relations of interest. (For Bentham, whether I'm a good person or not, or from one culture or another, is less important to my good or bad conduct than whether I'm in a position where I can abuse my position without penalty.) It was an aesthetic and moral mistake because some interests, or more precisely some pleasures, are higher than others and if pursued will make me a better character given to better conduct; and some are lower and if pursued are going to make me a worse character given to worse conduct. (For Bentham, pushpin, a children's game, was as good as poetry.) It was a political mistake because people's characters in a representative democracy need to be adequately educated: otherwise democracy can become very dangerous, even tyrannical, and the dangers are sufficient, Mill notoriously argued, that voting should be weighted by education. (For Bentham, it is enough that voters are ready and able to be watchful, and their representatives exposed to the public eye in the commission of duties.)

Mill's broader art and science of government, then, of which political economy was a part, aimed at the development of virtuous characters: this was best done through liberty and would result in greater happiness. Bentham's broader art and science of government, of which political economy was a part, was motivated by the greatest happiness principle to better arrange relations among people as it found them. Because utility doesn't translate directly to law and policy this meant in practice an emphasis on the four "subordinate" ends of legislation: security, subsistence, abundance, and equality.[65] Bentham was serious about utility, or happiness, and thought it a real thing. In fact, utility is made up of the only real things known directly and immediately to all sentient creatures: pain and pleasure. But twentieth-century economic literature's caricature of Bentham as an outmoded substantivist relying on an outmoded metaphysics, with a normative project based in this crude materiality, is false. Much of Bentham's political economy is indeed classical and substantivist, focused on promoting subsistence and abundance, with abundance as the guarantee of subsistence, in terms of material wealth. Yet his more general art and science of government is about facilitating a regime of prudence and probity aimed at detecting and eliminating waste. The regime demands a language for comparison and calculability, which is utility: a pragmatic and relative rather than absolute standard, a way to deploy economy as an end and means of rule. This emphasis on calculability is what motivates Marshall, correctly, to refer to Bentham as a relentless logician.

In one respect, Bentham's language of utility eliminates virtue per se as a concern. Identifying and promoting excellence, even in the mild and relatively democratic way that Smith does, implies potentially imperious judgment and discrimination. Bentham inaugurates the more radical liberalism of modern economic thought. Everyone and everything is leveled: each to count for one, and none for more than one.[66] In Bentham's hands no goal or desire is indicted in and of itself: pleasure is a good for the one anticipating it, no matter what it is, and should be accepted as simply given by everyone else. It is different if actual pursuit of the pleasure causes pain to another: as in classical and neoclassical economics; consent is a good indicator of whether that's the case. Not long before writing publicly on usury Bentham wrote privately on "sodomy"; both are disparaging terms describing consensual activities that Bentham considered not just harmless but beneficial.[67] Bentham has to deal with the problem that public opinion about these and other practices he thinks should be decriminalized itself involves pain and pleasure; antipathy toward religious and sexual minorities, for example, is a preference held by many that, apart from the effects of its satisfaction, is not indictable. His radical reform approach identifies and calls out prejudicial rhetoric and criticizes the projection of one's own likes and dislikes onto the social order as a whole. He substitutes a neutral terminology and a standard of cost and benefit, which, along with a study of social cause and effect, can bring what he takes to be real waste into view – for example, the waste of punishing non-crimes at all or of punishing real crimes more than necessary – so as to eliminate that waste.

In another respect, then, utility elevates the virtue of economy that is central to the political-economic tradition to a supreme principle of individual and collective conduct. At the individual level this exposes a conundrum: how to judge what is waste for another? At the collective level, which for Bentham is nothing but an aggregate of individuals, this becomes not only a theme for radical reform but the very means of coordinating conduct, through a regime of incentives and disincentives. Bentham's political-economic writings do share some traditional ideas with his contemporaries, of economy as individual virtue and of the need to inculcate it, especially among the poor. Yet usury is condemned by others, like Smith, for encouraging "prodigals." Concerning these spendthrift borrowers, Bentham takes a different tack more consistent with his general outlook:

> I should look upon it as incumbent on me to place in a fair light the reasons there may be for doubting, how far, with regard to a person arrived at the age of discretion, third persons may be competent judges, which of two pains may be of greater force and value to him, the present pain of restraining his present desires, or the future contingent pain he may be exposed to suffer from the want to which

the expence of gratifying these desires may hereafter have reduced him.[68]

In other words, "who is to judge"? Individuals have what economists now call different "discount rates" when weighing the present against the future. That is a matter of their own preference schedules, so it is no less rational for them to have a much higher regard for the present than the future. As Bentham writes in *An Introduction to the Principles of Morals and Legislation*, some say "passion does not calculate." But that is "not true ... Men calculate, some with less exactness, indeed, some with more: but all men calculate. I would not say, that even a madman does not calculate."[69] This continuous calculation, this more or less well-tuned economic rationality, Bentham calls "interest." It is the ground, motor, and effect of a governmental apparatus that assumes, as textbook economics does, that "'people respond to incentives – the rest is commentary.'"[70]

According to Jon Elster, our model of allocative choice is ultimately theomorphic; the first example of true rational allocative choice is Gottfried Leibniz's God, who works with finite means to create the best of all possible worlds.[71] If Bentham secularizes this into a worldly legislative science with a worldly maximand, it is to ensure that aptitude is maximized and expense minimized ("maximize" and "minimize" were coined by Bentham).[72] One way to maximize governmental aptitude and minimize cost is for the governed to take on more government; this is the secret of the efficiency of the Panopticon (the inmates watch themselves because they don't know when their unseen guard is watching them), and is how Bentham conceives of the market. For Bentham as for Smith, the "bon marché or the cheapness of provisions, and the having the market well supplied with ... commodities" is an important part of police.[73] But, rather than a system of natural liberty, which for Bentham is an obvious contradiction in terms, "nonsense upon stilts,"[74] Bentham characterizes the market as "indirect legislation." He relies, like Smith, on the spontaneous action of buyers and sellers. For Bentham the legislator, by constructing the needed field of security (of property, publicity, etc.), effectively enlists players in the market as agents, policing one another through competition in order better to promote the governmental goals of Smith's desired cheapness and plenty.[75]

The twentieth and twenty-first-century figure of allocative choice – what the literary critic Jane Elliott calls the "microeconomic mode" – is able to forget the way that it operates as a mode of self-government and government of others, that is, as an ethics and a politics. Until, that is, it is reminded of this by the conflict between economic rationalists and their behavioral critics. Interest, in the microeconomic mode, remains a relationship, but a very peculiar one. Its ethical and political aims and consequences are both obscured and achieved by reconceiving ethics and politics as individual ends, as preferences to be satisfied. As Elliott writes:

> we act out of interest not simply when we serve narrowly self-directed goals ... but rather whenever we approach choices as unfolding within this sort of microeconomy of costs and benefits, means and ends. As a form of imaginative interiority, interest is what propels the subject to experience the world as continually eliciting rational allocative choice.[76]

Bentham shows how individuals who experience the world this way are eminently governable. Later nineteenth-century economics took from Bentham the core of his art and science of government, his concept of interest, to develop the microeconomic mode. Refined into a science of conduct, refined further into a neo-positivist science of choice, economics forgot its political and ethical origins. What is from Smith through Mill a full-blown political philosophy concerned with the problem of domination, what is still in Bentham's own politics a spur to independence of taste, radical reform, and democratic accountability, the microeconomic mode transforms. Economic rationality centered on choice refines into a theme for managerial inventiveness, blind to domination and blind to the public as such, its route smoothed by the potential limitlessness of the imaginative interiority of a new interest.

4

Economics as Politics

Economic science does its politics through a disavowal of
politics. The rise of rational allocative choice has played a
central role in this disavowal. Granted, before the ascendancy
of choice Jean-Baptiste Say and other first-generation political
economists of the early nineteenth century were concerned to
distinguish their science from the study of political relations
and political systems, and to declare its applicability in
different times and places and its compatibility with different
political regimes. And they were concerned to distinguish a
broad array of virtues from the narrow band they associated
with wealth-building. But they were well aware, unlike
modern economists, that theirs was an ethical and trans-
valuative project: against a range of traditional views that
cast moral suspicion on accumulation, they argued for a
positive relationship between economy, its wealth-building,
and a range of virtues. Political economists were frank about
their science's political role: its need to inform a branch
of the broader art of government. Political economy was
an explicitly pedagogical endeavor. It informed the self-
government of the governed – mainly the growing middle
classes but reaching out to the laboring majority – and it
aimed to educate mostly upper-class governors in its counter-
intuitive lessons. Its focus was to promote virtues specific to
productive self-interest and to the proper political-economic
coordination of that interest.

The development by political economists and their contemporaries of a broadly utilitarian political and ethical language

of *interest* was a significant achievement. The achievement was to give theoretical grounding to an Enlightenment program that joined individual virtue to social progress through nascent social science, able to marshal arguments against conservatives and revolutionaries alike. Political economy provided a new story about contemporary class society that saw it as conventional but mostly necessary, fundamentally stable and interdependent, yet in need of often radical if gradual political and social reform in the public interest. Political economy embraced, even as it moderated and redirected, republican demands to curb domination and arbitrary power, by way of prioritizing and mobilizing the secured rights of modern liberalism. Independence and self-command and their democratization were very much on the agenda, if not for their own sake then as furthering the umbrella goal of aggregate prosperity and happiness. (Consider how many economists talk in a more value-free idiom today about women's education in poor countries, or diversity, equity, and inclusion in rich countries, as contributors to economic growth.)

There was no pretense in British political economy that its project was not a political and ethical one, even as it declared its independence from State and Church. Well into the twentieth century many of political economy's most prominent practitioners were religious non-conformists (a.k.a. dissenters, Free Churchers), and the young discipline's sometimes explicitly "civilizing" project both at home and abroad could readily merge with a missionary one. No classical political economist would see their art and science as the whole of the civilizing project or as comprehending all of conduct: political economy studied a crucial but limited commercial sphere of life, even if the science was thought to be applicable beyond modern Britain to all times and places. The pushback against cosmopolitan assumptions and aims, which was mostly from the continent and across the Atlantic, was significant and acknowledged. Historical and institutional reactions within the discipline objected to claims of universality, insisting that the science as it developed was appropriate to some contexts more than others, or designed to help some parties and regions at the expense of others.[1]

In the twentieth century and beyond, the economic mainstream took a very different critical approach to that of the classical era, in more direct opposition to historical and institutional perspectives. Animated by epistemic virtues informing new protocols of scientific objectivity,[2] economics has worked to purify itself from the taint of politics and ethics. Like other positivist social sciences, economics sees politics and ethics as a kind of contamination rooted in individual scientists' "biases" and thus requiring self-control on the part of the scientist.[3] But what are called "values" and rigorously distinguished from "facts" are not matters of personal character, and they are always already built-in to language and practice, including the language and practice of the human sciences.[4] Purification has gone hand-in-glove with greater insistence on the universality of economic science, not only for different institutional contexts, but as speaking to all conduct. The most ardent and successful purifier and universalizer was the young Lionel Robbins, who was raised in a Strict Baptist farming family, and who rose quickly following the First World War to become chair of the Economics department of the London School of Economics at the age of thirty.[5] Robbins provided a lasting definition of economics, still probably the most widely cited in the discipline: "Economics is the science which studies human behaviour as a relationship between ends and scarce means which have alternative uses."[6] Robbins' definition thus pointed to more or less rational allocative choice as an "aspect" of all behavior.

Robbins' stated intent in the essay where he developed this definition, *An Essay on the Nature and Significance of Economic Science* (1932, revised 1935), was a kind of modesty, especially with regard to the capacity of economic science to render policy advice. In a sense, he was attempting finally to root out the "political" left over from political economy's transition to economics, and to reserve the term "political economy" for the explicitly value-laden business of economic policy. He attacked the utilitarian, and so putatively normative and unscientific, practice of welfare economics, so long as the latter disguised itself as something that could be read off, as it were, from economics proper. Robbins was firm, following Adam Smith's friend and contemporary

David Hume, that one cannot derive "ought" statements from "is" statements, and he was worried that many of his colleagues were doing just that with their economics. Economic science should have nothing to say about ends, just about the more or less rational choice of scarce means with respect to given ends. The rationality of rational choice on this view is completely formal and not substantive; there are no economic ends, Robbins repeats, just more or less economical means to ends.

In a somewhat curmudgeonly review of the essay, especially coming as it did from a new friend and fellow theorist of allocative choice,[7] Robbins' American contemporary Frank Knight accused Robbins, a decidedly clear and concise thinker, of intellectual sloppiness and rhetorical excess. Knight, who at the University of Chicago taught James Buchanan, Milton Friedman, and George Stigler, among others (Paul Samuelson was an undergraduate), shared Robbins' price/subjective value orientation, but he was more of a skeptic than many of his students and colleagues about the reach and significance of their discipline. According to Knight's review, Robbins' discussion "centers in means and ends, with no recognition of the paradox of such concepts appearing in a pure science." And there is moreover "serious confusion" in the essay about ends: as Knight says, "all 'ends' involved in [an economic problem] are quantitatively comparable; that is, qualitatively, there is but one end." Knight takes exception to Robbins' dismissal of money as "'mere means,'" when "money is largely an end, subjectively and functionally." Ultimately, "The categorical distinction between judgments of 'is' and 'ought' which Robbins stresses so often ... simply cannot be maintained."[8] Building on Knight, one might say that to approach a problem in economic terms is hardly to accept ends as given and to leave them untouched. In fact ends, when considered according to economic reasoning, are no longer ends as normally understood: they are not qualitatively distinct non-divisible things to be effectively accomplished or not. Instead all "ends" are rendered commensurable and subject to partial or total trade-off.[9] Some economists (most emphatically the Austrian tradition) object strongly to anyone other than individuals, especially state actors, thinking they are in a position to make their tradeoffs for them.[10] But surprisingly few economists – Knight is an early exception – notice how peculiar and consequential it is to assume this commensurability at the level of the individual, and to insist that this mode of choosing is what is going on when people act.[11] With a broadly shared and putatively neutral insistence on commensurable choice,[12] economics transgresses limits placed on classical political economy by the latter's comparative self-awareness.

Knight's objections open the way, among other things, to a performative understanding of economics. In another piece written in response to a critique of Robbins, he wrote that "social 'science' itself is a social phenomenon of … communication aimed at agreement." In fact, "it seems doubtful whether the term 'science' should be used without warning qualifications, to characterize discourse, which must explain the discourse itself, and which is addressed to its own subject matter, and must change, and is primarily intended to change, that subject-matter."[13] That Knight was sympathetic to the ways in which Robbins' work aimed to recast economic theory and practice – both were at the time old-style liberals opposed to national planning measures taken or proposed in their countries during the Great Depression – didn't stop him from noticing that their joint enterprise was political in this way, and that Robbins protested too much that theirs was a value-free science.

As the political scientist Timothy Mitchell has argued in our own time, one shouldn't suppose that economics either gets a world prior to or apart from it right, or gets it wrong. Instead, one should recognize that economics "operates from within the sociotechnical world, not from someplace outside it." Think of economics as providing "a set of instruments of calculation and other technical devices, whose strength lies … in their usefulness for organizing sociotechnical processes, such as markets."[14] In other words, economics does a lot to help make the world it ostensibly studies, and in doing so is productive of numerous arrangements and effects that are much more adequate to some human ends than they are to others.

The struggles of the global pandemic of 2020 illustrate well the consequences of a world-making that channels government through allocative choice. Public health authorities are helpless in the face of the rhetorical elevation and validation of individual cost/benefit calculations, and in the United States these authorities have sometimes contributed to the problem by attempting to mobilize the rational choice language-game rather than fight it. They have, for example, "sold" masks and vaccines as smart measures for protecting oneself and one's family, rather than initiate a conversation about small but necessary measures of solidarity, duty, sacrifice, and so on, for a world in common in which it is ultimately impossible to disentangle one's own interests from others, for a health commons from which there is, as it were, no exit.[15] In Robbins' era, by way of contrast, the status of infectious disease protection as public rather than private good was crystal clear: "In urban conditions the failure of one individual to conform to certain sanitary requirements may involve all the others in an epidemic." This is only one of the "obvious limitations on the possibility of formulating ends in price offers" (*NS*, 144).

These "obvious limitations" on doing things with prices are regularly transgressed by contemporary economists working in the microeconomic mode, from across the political spectrum. Public bads are redefined as negative "externalities," as by-products of transactions between disassociated allocative choosers who need to be and could be incentivized to ameliorate the situation, if only the externalities were brought in, that is, properly priced. Even a problem as inescapably common and of such incalculable dimensions as the unfolding climate catastrophe is approached in this way. William Nordhaus, winner of the 2018 Nobel Prize, was a pioneer and is a veteran of climate economics, much of which generates models that attempt to put a price on carbon emissions as a guide to taxes and other coordinated abatement strategies. Nordhaus recognizes, among other difficulties, that uncertainties surrounding factors making up the "social cost of carbon" are daunting.[16] Critics, even those at peace with the idea of computing any number of commensurable costs and benefits, wonder how something that has already demonstrated cascading effects, and thus renders untold death and destruction an ever nearer-term possibility, can be represented as a cost at all. Consider further the world-making performed by the dominance and pervasiveness of economic discourse, such that the climate crisis is thought of as a policy problem in the first place, with solutions largely dependent on the discipline's modeling and management.

Economics is a vast enterprise, and there are multiple possible routes to a genealogy of the ideal of rational economic choice, which is in any case not the aim of this chapter. The question here is instead that of the political *significance* of commensurable choice. Robbins' work, especially his early and influential essay, is an excellent prism through which to view the sources and effects of the refinement of economics' "micro" foundations. There is a danger that a focus on Robbins, the avatar of "LSE economics" (with Chicago, Virginia, and Austrian economists contributing minor chords) appears parochial to mainstream economists, who might be much more skeptical of markets. Also, many theoretically inclined economists who rely on choice have entirely abandoned the last vestiges of intro-spection, and might wonder what the lineage described here has to do with them. But strict choice-as-behavior theorists will still speak of preferences and see choice (perfectly reasonably, they *are* economists) as interacting with prices, and known, un-imputed prices actually are fully commensu-rable with one another, unlike any number of other things. In so far as a more narrow "consistency-only" approach to rationality is then extended as a starting point for thinking about rational conduct beyond actual pricing markets, as it usually is (by thinking of other things informing behavior in terms of preferences and prices), questions about the micro-economic mode and its political significance return. The political-theoretical implications of economic rationality that I consider here follow from any extended attachment to the choice paradigm, whether more or less introspective, more or less state-friendly, etc.

Some may read this chapter as just another critique of the economist as engineer or policy scientist, often aimed at neo-Keynesian Paul Samuelson and other postwar theorists and practitioners attuned to market failure and the potentials of state capacity by their experiences of economic collapse and war. This is a misreading. My political-theoretical approach is not entirely unrelated to that critique, but my lopsided focus on the kinds of economic theory that *make* that critique should give pause to any such assimilation. There is nothing wrong with policy science per se; of course, policy should be informed by science. But policy does not exhaust politics, other knowledges can reasonably inform policy besides policy science, and certainly no one policy science can reasonably claim to be the indispensable one. The Robbins approach, as well as many "new welfare" and "neo-institutional" reactions to or consequences from it, easily leads to these latter transgressions; Robbins' own critique of policy science simply reinforces the ping-ponging between subjective value and objective science that buttresses economics' antipolitical politics. None of what I argue here applies to economists in the classical, old-institutional, or historical modes, or to many cautious mathematical or empirical scientists in the neoclassical mode. But it very much applies not only to economists of the Right, but to their center-Left opposites, who may have had more impact than their adversaries in reframing and thus limiting political horizons, particularly on the Left.[17] And it applies above all to the foundational lessons in the centrality of choice and trade-off that textbook economics has been teaching millions of non-economic experts in other disciplines.[18] What I argue with respect to Robbins follows from a hegemonic conception of microeconomic rationality, one found across important technical and normative differences, which is still dominant now in several fields and fundamental to their teachings. This should not be surprising, because Robbins' own relatively catholic approach to rationality helped establish this hegemony.

Although many commentators over the years, including Knight, have stressed Robbins' Austrian influences, his more direct inspiration was Philip Wicksteed;[19] we can trace a line back through Wicksteed to William Stanley Jevons, both of whom were nonconformists, specifically Unitarians (Wicksteed was a Unitarian minister). Jevons looked to Jeremy Bentham for the foundations of his science, deployed the language of "choice," and was one of the first to drop the "political" from political economy. Robbins relied on Wicksteed and a continuing dialogue with Austrian economics to develop a more analytically pure science. This science would, by Robbins' lights, purge itself of utilitarianism by more fully developing the subjective theory of value, that is, by advancing the increasingly broadly recognized, and newly named, "neoclassical" revolution in economics dating from the 1870s (now conventionally jointly attributed to the "marginalist" work of Jevons of Manchester, Léon Walras of Lausanne, and Carl Menger of Vienna).[20] The irony with regard to utilitarianism is that this entire edifice, of value and choice grounded in individual taste and calculation, is essentially built from foundations borrowed from Bentham's political thought.

Robbins' essay provides insight as to how the attempted purging of politics and ethics from economics helps to constitute a distinctive antipolitical political theory, a kind of stunted utilitarianism. The idea of economics as stunted utilitarianism is a familiar one, but in a different sense from that meant here. Many from both within and outside the discipline have accused economists of promoting a ruinously impoverished conception of welfare.[21] A more robust utilitarianism is explicitly on the agenda for those who want to, as it were, bring happiness back to economics through new economic performance measures.[22] Yet the stunted utilitarianism I allude to is not defective in a normative sense: the problem, again, is not so much that economics is normatively thin or empty, or that it doesn't get things right. The problem instead is how modern economics takes up, in disguised and limited form, a variation on what utilitarianism originally was: not first and foremost a normative or empirical theory of society but rather more fundamentally a theory of the art and science of government, of the conduct of conduct.[23]

Art is practical: prior to, or in the course of doing, it entails deciding what to do in the sense of what ends to pursue. The science paired with art, a practical science of cause and effect,[24] is technical; it recommends means and helps decide what to do only in the sense of how to pursue ends given by art (unless it pronounces the ends impossible).[25] Classical utilitarian art and science is a project of rational administration that claims to better harmonize ends and means already given by individual schedules of pleasures and pains and a set of given environmental constraints. The science of economics, which substitutes ordinal preferences for measurable pleasures and pains, is utilitarianism's most politically salient disciplinary offspring. Bentham wrote very little on morality per se, and what his bowdlerizing literary executor John Bowring assembled under this heading looks a lot like economic advising.[26] The idea is that "deontologists" would help individuals see distant consequences, so that they could better harmonize their practices and thus better maximize whatever gave them utility.

Bentham's broader art and science aimed at promoting utility as a common idiom through which to connect and harmonize otherwise conflicting interests. Such a project was proudly and explicitly performative, "(s)triving to cut a new road through the wilds of jurisprudence."[27] For Bentham, the theory of motivation that economics took up, the theory that was refined into rational allocative choice, was the basis for politically adjusting and re-directing legal and reputational sanctions to tie one's duty – for example, not to harm others – to one's interest. Thus a properly crafted penal law forbidding a practice is essentially an advertised sanction that its accompanying penalty puts on the practice. The price of the sanction needs to be sufficiently high to disincentivize the practice but not so high as to be wastefully punishing.[28] In this way, institutional arrangements could be reformed and conduct could be better coordinated with the aid of multiple forms of expertise. All kinds of crafts and professions might be enlisted or consulted for help with this government-by-sanction, from printers to physicians.

Although Bentham's politics was implicitly therapeutic and explicitly managerial, he increasingly relied on democratic forms and their activation in public space to combat "sinister" interests, that is, the interests of dominant establishments at odds with the aggregate interests of the governed. Economics, by contrast, often acknowledges public space only as something to be administered: by way of economic management, or, for anti-policy purists, by way of better or worse choices, based on their science of choice, of rules constraining choices. Microeconomic foundations tend to elevate subjectivity and objectivity at the expense of everything in between, in abstraction from the social and at the expense of the space of politics. The apparent humility, with regard to ends, of the discipline defined by Robbins turns out to be only apparent, as this economics can effectively disenchant alternative politics and alternative knowledges, and elevate itself as a distinctive and necessary all-purpose expertise.[29] Economics' utilitarianism is stunted in comparison to its classical forebear because participation in representative government, for example, loses its luster and even its legitimacy,[30] and because the importance of disciplinary expertise narrows from multiple fields to one. A close reading of Robbins' essay betrays how an increasingly technical science of economics can double as the only indispensable practical art.

Economists fiercely criticize one another over microeconomic foundations and the content and viability of the rationality assumption. However, whether "subjective" and "objective" values (if the latter are recognized) can be linked up, whether rationality is more or less about optimization, and whether rationality is at all descriptive of behavior, are all less important than the common tendency in these debates as well as in textbook economics to make choice foundational. Every economist invested in the centrality of choice – every economist invested in the story that sees valuing choice as the motive power of social action and interaction – is committed at a minimum to the idea that rational action is a matter of action driven by a commensurable balance of "either this or that," driven by valuation, where this or that can better satisfy the valuing unit, from its perspective. The notion that what it is to act rationally is to be driven by such a balance might seem uncontroversial but it is actually quite distinctive and peculiar in relation to other traditions of thinking about rationality. It suggests that reason is monologic rather than dialogic.[31] And it suggests that even monologic instrumental reason itself responds less to a problem of some sort, to what is called for in any situation (how do I get out of this heat? how do we defend against this threat?), and more to an imagined schedule of subjectively grounded valuation, as it connects with choice-shaping incentives and disincentives.

To make choice foundational in this way is ultimately to be turned toward the idea that rational – or systematically and so predictably irrational – conduct is manageable conduct. Whatever ends a chooser might seem to have, the idea of subjective value suggests that they ultimately have only one end, and that economists' knowledge is always well suited to help them both discover and pursue it, whether they are "choosing" as an individual, as a household, as a firm, or as a state.[32] That there is within economics a strong current questioning the limits of economic science makes little difference to this framework. Because the strain of economic knowledge founded on subjective utility and choice, despite its protestations to political innocence and despite the intentions of many practitioners, sets itself up rhetorically as all-purpose knowledge, even a "negative" economics questioning its own usefulness can serve to delegitimate other specialist advice, not to mention more democratic forms of expertise. Robbins' own understanding of, and aims for, economic rationality are modest indeed. But that doesn't stop his essay from having far-reaching political implications.

Choice and balance

Robbins was at pains to purge utilitarianism from the discipline, ironically by attempting to give analytic specification to what Knight called "essentially the 'utility mechanics' of Jevons," or the "quasi-mathematical theory of price and utility."[33] (Despite its enormous footprint and continuing textbook dominance, the reader is reminded by Knight not to take Robbins' characterization of economic science to exhaust the discipline, either then or now.) *The Nature and Significance of Economic Science* was written up from Robbins' lectures at the London School of Economics in the early 1930s. Behind Robbins' famous definition in terms of allocative choice is the urge to purge ethics and politics from economics proper, to outline a purely positive science of human behavior. And what economics studies about human behavior – that is, the relationship between ends and means that have alternative uses – applies, it seems, to all kinds of conduct regarding all kinds of ends and means. Economics can study an aspect of everything anyone does; it can study all behavior looked at from a certain point of view. Just as there are no economic ends, according to Robbins, there is no specifically economic sphere. Others want to say that economics is about material life or about basic as opposed to higher ends. No: there is nothing more carnal than spiritual about economic life; it can concern the allocation of so much money toward food or the theater, or the allocation of so much time between labor or prayer. Whatever the something, and whatever the "this or that," if some individual or society or other unit uses so much of something for this, they can't use as much for that. This is textbook economic choice; one cannot, simply put, have one's cake and eat it too (*NS*, 24–45). Trade-offs are the way of the world, and economists are simply bringing this unhappy fact of scarcity to light. Robbins quips: "Your economist is a true tragedian" (*NS*, 30).

Robbins comes back repeatedly, throughout the essay, to the value-neutrality of economics. As he clarifies in a late retrospective lecture, any "political" economy is necessarily normative; there is nothing wrong with doing political economy, but it is crucial that it be acknowledged that any such endeavor is not the applied economics it might appear to be. Unlike economics, political economy in this sense is not a positive science and must not be said to follow from any science at all, as that would illegitimately pronounce what ought to be on the basis of what is.[34] If economics is not a policy science, though, what is the point? What is the significance of economics? Robbins was, after all, writing his foundational essay during the Depression, during a time when many readers were looking for answers; they were looking for social science to help with pressing social problems. Economics, it turns out, is actually vital for policy and for decisions of all sorts at all levels. According to Robbins economists can, with their science, point out to any choosing unit, including the public as a whole, via their government, a kind of inconsistency. Economists can show how the use of such-and-such means to accomplish end A might end up unintentionally subverting the achievement of another given end B: consider, for example, how in many circumstances the protection of domestic industries through tariffs produces a rise in prices. If the public, knowing this about these unintended and otherwise unforeseen consequences, decides to protect itself as producers at the expense of itself as consumers, economics has nothing to say about it; but economics can prevent this or another decision from being made blindly, in ignorance of the consequences (*NS*, 152–158). Notice how far, at least on the face of things, this is from classical political economy. Economics appears to be at once more and less ambitious than its predecessor. On the one hand, economics applies to any allocative choice scenario whatsoever; it is not limited to commercial life. On the other hand, economics is apparently not at all directive; it is not, it seems, telling (or really even advising) any individual or state or other economic unit what to do.

Robbins was instrumental in bringing Friedrich Hayek to LSE, and the essay's first preface acknowledges "especial indebtedness to the works of Professor Ludwig von Mises" (*NS* xv–xvi). But the essentials of Robbins' perspective can be gleaned from his fellow Englishman Wicksteed and the latter's far more prolix *The Common Sense of Political Economy*, first published in 1910 (and also acknowledged in the preface). In 1932, the same year as the publication of the first edition of *Nature and Significance*, Robbins edited Wicksteed's text for republication. His introduction to Wicksteed (dated October 1932) is full of praise. Robbins credits his predecessor with refusing to paper over the discontinuity between economics and the older political economy in the manner of the bridge-building Alfred Marshall, the dominant figure in the Anglophone political economy of the early twentieth century. Instead, Wicksteed built new foundations.[35]

The new economics would famously put individuals' marginally sensitive decisions at the root of price-formation and the discipline as a whole, overturning classical conceptions of value, scarcity, and the source and meaning of economic laws. And for Robbins and his colleagues at LSE it would provide a framework of great analytical power and universal application that could show up the wrongheadedness of a variety of intervening Continental and American historical and institutional approaches.[36] Wicksteed was a leader for all of these purposes as he had, early in his venture into economics, written a trenchant critique of Karl Marx's *Capital* from the new subjective-value perspective.[37]

Wicksteed's own greatest debt was to Jevons. It was careful study of Jevons' *Theory of Political Economy* (first published 1871) that persuaded Wicksteed, an earnest social reformer, of the dangers of some radical proposals and of the broader significance of political economy for understanding contemporary society. Jevons in turn was a key figure in the centering of choice. He was a mathematician and logician and is widely acknowledged as one of the progenitors of the so-called marginal or neoclassical revolution.[38] Jevons had worked in Australia and his writing makes typical settler-colonial reference to "savage" shortsightedness.[39] Thus economic rationality with Jevons (as with his contemporary Marshall) carried across the classical/neoclassical divide a conception of civilizational discipline that is still echoed more or less faintly in the development, behavioral, and public finance literatures, among other places.

In the preface to the second edition (1879) of *The Theory of Political Economy* Jevons writes: "Among minor alterations, I may mention the substitution for the name Political Economy of the single convenient term Economics. I cannot help thinking that it would be well to discard, as quickly as possible, the old troublesome double-worded name of our Science." The new term has "authority of usage from the time of Aristotle." Jevons credits Marshall, among others, for adopting it, and notes that the French, ahead of the English in this and other respects, have long referred to "*la science économique*" (*TPE*, xiv). Jevons is explicit in *TPE* that he is re-founding the discipline, and he is consistently hostile to "the principal doctrines of the Ricardo-Mill Economics" (*TPE*, li). The latter had hardened into a dogma from the "noxious influence of authority," which impedes the free inquiry necessary to scientific advance (*TPE*, 275). Jevons doesn't spell out here what is "troublesome" about political economy as a name for economics, but there are strong hints in the presentation. He wants to model what was still known as a moral science on what were called the "physical" sciences,[40] and in particular on contemporary physics.[41] Key to the effort is the derivation of hypotheses from axioms of behavior of a fundamental atomic unit, the utility-maximizing individual.

Although Jevons indulges in Millian talk of "higher" and "lower" pleasures, the aim throughout is to take individuals' specific pleasures and pains as given, and as the motive force of choice. As he notes in response to a concern raised about the first edition, Jevons had originally written that "gaming is a sure way to lose utility" because he had taken "no account of the utility – that is, the pleasure – attaching to the pursuit of gaming itself," but only attended to "the commercial loss or gain." Yet if a person "prefers" to run the substantial risk of losing money rather than do something else with their funds, if they are "so devoid of other tastes" that gambling is the best use for their money, then "economically speaking, there is nothing further to be said. The question then becomes a moral, legislative, or political one" (*TPE*, 160). Economics, then, for Jevons, is fully distinct from politics and ethics, and on the very grounds, the democratization and liberalization of taste, established by the master theorist of the pleasure/pain calculus, Jeremy Bentham.

In the preface to the second edition Jevons confirms what is clear from his first chapters, that Bentham's philosophy is the foundation of his economics: "As to Bentham's ideas, they are adopted as the starting-point of the theory given in this work" (*TPE*, xxvi). Bentham's calculus is key to Jevons' main purpose and most lasting achievement: to make Anglophone political economy into a mathematical science.[42] The essentials are laid out already in a paper presented in 1862 and published in 1866, "Brief Account of a General Mathematical Theory of Political Economy." There Jevons presents what he calls a "true theory of economy," which "can only be attained by going back to the great springs of human action – *the feelings of pleasure and pain*." Feelings are capable of "more or less"; thus they are "quantities capable of scientific treatment" (*TPE*, Appendix III, 304, emphasis in original).

This "more or less," this commensurability of feeling, is how Jevons can make foundational what he calls the "act" of choice: "Our estimation of the comparative amounts of feeling is performed in the act of choice or volition. Our choice of one course out of two or more proves that, in our estimation, this course promises the greatest balance of pleasure" (*TPE*, Appendix III, 304). The starting point of the new economics is *introspective*; it grounds all worldly activity in the interior of the individual, in a profound reversal of Smithian encounter and the classical tradition's social focus. No innovations in the choice tradition, no turning on pleasure and pain as part of an outmoded metaphysics or energetics, no replacement of cardinal measures by ordinal ones, no worries about whether the economic actor has a rational or an irrational psychology or whether psychology even matters, no avoidance of value-talk altogether, changes this basic antipolitical course. One of the neoclassical tradition's more impressive feats since Robbins, among many, has been to create a whole new "political economy": not Robbins' policy science but instead a subdiscipline of economics that overlaps with similarly oriented work in political science. That subdiscipline asks "what are the foundations of politics and institutions more broadly, either in general, or these in particular"? The answer given by those working with strictly neoclassical tools is that the institutions in question are the benign or malign product or byproduct of allocative choosing, and that they in turn shape subsequent choices. Institutions might be created, for example, to save on choosing agents' "transaction costs." Put differently, politics and institutions are imagined away so that they can be brought back into being theoretically, in a kind of scientific refinement of the state-of-nature rhetorical framing of early modern natural-rights jurisprudence. This way of thinking is very foreign to the classical political-economic tradition and its understanding of the institutional and pedagogical framework assumed and required to produce anything like rational allocative choosers in the first place.[43]

The concept of balance, and its capacity to establish equivalences between vanishingly small bits of different goods or services, provides for Jevons the basis for "the most important law of the whole theory" (what he called "final" and others would call marginal utility), and its grounding of a theory of exchange and market equivalences. The "coefficient of utility" is based on the idea that every "appetite or sense is more or less rapidly satiated"; it is "the ratio between the last increment or infinitely small supply of the object, and the increment of pleasure which it occasions." Different goods and different individuals have different utility functions (*TPE*, Appendix III, 305–306). The mathematical theory, which incorporates the complex dynamics of foresight, generates a new understanding of labor and capital and economic process generally. And it ultimately comes down to choice.

By resolving choice into a "balance" of pleasure over pain as spring of action, and by noting diminishing returns from accumulation of the same objects of pleasure, Jevons goes back to Bentham, and specifically acknowledges Bentham's

"Table of the Springs of Action" (1817) and the 1822 "Codification Proposal, addressed by Jeremy Bentham to All Nations professing Liberal Opinions" (*TPE*, xxvi).[44] Bentham authored these well after he had largely left political economy behind. The Table and elements of the Proposal recall the foundational work for his general art and science of government that Bentham published in *An Introduction to the Principles of Morals and Legislation* (1789). Jevons cites the famous opening to Bentham's *Introduction* toward the end of his own introduction: "'Nature ... has placed mankind under the governance of two sovereign masters – *pain and pleasure* ... On the one hand the standard of right and wrong, on the other the chain of causes and effects, are fastened to their throne'" (*TPE*, 24, emphasis in Bentham's original). One might read the elaboration of pain and pleasure in Bentham's Table as about cause and effect, or Bentham's theory of motivation, and their elaboration in his Proposal as about right and wrong. But for Bentham the two are necessarily of a piece.

We find Jevons' final or marginal utility, his theory of value, in the Proposal. There, Bentham offers himself to a global network of republican revolutionaries and reformers as a drafter of complete codes of law grounded in the principle of utility. Laws must make their rationales clear, and these rationales must always be that they are conducive to happiness, and happiness consists in more pleasure and less pain. Thus Bentham writes of the "value" of a pleasure or pain. "But," writes Bentham, "the magnitude of the pleasure produced by [the object] does not encrease in so great a ratio as that in which the magnitude of the cause encreases." He gives the example of money, and how this law of diminishing returns might not be evident with small sums; yet it is apparent that the unexpected receipt of a second identical large sum of money will not bring as much pleasure as the first. According to Bentham, "it will then be a matter of mathematical certainty that the dimunition can not have been made to take place in the case of the greatest quantity without having been made to take place, in a proportionable amount, in the case of the several lesser quantities." And: "As it is with money, so it is with all other sources or causes of pleasure" (Bentham gives the example of honorary ribbons).[45]

We find Jevons' balance, the motive for an act of choice, in Bentham's theory of interest as given by the Table. There is according to Bentham no such thing as a disinterested act; all conduct proceeds from interest. Following an assertion of identity between the good and pleasure, the language of balance is introduced with respect to the motive meaning of "interest":

> It is said *to be a man's interest that* the act, the event, or the state of things in question should have place, in so far as it is supposed that – upon, and in consequence of, its having place – *good*, to a greater *value*, will be possessed by him than in the contrary case. *(I)nterest* ... corresponds to *a balance* on the side of *good*.[46]

Bentham's account is identical to Jevons' picture of conduct, the choice of which "promises the greatest balance of pleasure." Ironically, though, Jevons' theory in its original presentation bows to the authority of John Stuart Mill in shrinking from the full implications of Bentham's scheme. Unlike Bentham's economy of pleasure and pain, for Jevons "economy does not treat of all human motives" such as those arising from "conscience, compassion, or from some moral or religious source." Like Mill, Jevons originally understands these instead as "outstanding and disturbing forces" (*TPE*, Appendix III, 304), whereas for Bentham they are assimilated to reputation, sympathy (what in Jevons' time was becoming known as "altruism"),[47] and similarly less self-regarding summands of a unitary or monistic interest.[48] That the entries in this balance are pleasures and pains – they could be pluses and minuses of any sort – is far less important for the subsequent history of economics and its politics than that the entries are imagined[49] to be fully commensurable, if not by actual decision-makers in all but special circumstances, then certainly by economists themselves.

Pleasures, pains, and commensurability

In *Nature and Significance* Robbins is determined to free economics from utilitarianism. Given the origins and character of classical political economy, and given Jevons' systematic adaptation of Bentham, this was a tall order! But Robbins knew that if economics was utilitarian, it couldn't exactly be free of normativity, and he was determined to purify positive economic science. And Robbins was surrounded in his time by the explicit utilitarianism of contemporary welfare economics, of economists who were determined to use their science to enhance what they called "social utility," some version of classical utilitarianism's greatest good for the greatest number. This was according to Robbins especially prevalent in discussions of public finance, where proposals might explicitly aim at sizeable redistributions in service of equality so long as it could be argued that they didn't interfere with efficiency. In keeping with his value-free scientific standpoint Robbins writes in *Nature and Significance* that he has nothing against such proposals as "ethical postulates," but he is determined to free economics per se of such postulates. He goes so far as to state, one can't help but think disingenuously, that all this welfare work is "simply the accidental deposit of the historical association of English Economics with Utilitarianism" (*NS*, 141), and he is determined to keep them separated.

The original sin of welfare economics, and perhaps, for Robbins, of utilitarianism, was to make interpersonal utility calculations. Although Bentham certainly seems guilty of this, in so far as what he came to call the "greatest happiness principle" might imply a social aggregate, Robbins is aware, if not early on then in the course of his career, that for Bentham this is a convention, as "'you might as well add twenty apples to twenty pears.'"[50] And regardless, Bentham's emphasis on the priority of security (enshrined in the "disappointment-prevention principle") put serious limits on any application of marginal utility to redistributive measures. Jevons was explicit that such calculations are impossible. "The reader will find," he writes, "that there is never, in any single instance, an attempt made to compare the amount of feeling in one mind with that in another. I see no means by which such comparison can be accomplished" (*TPE*, 14). Jevons was a source for Robbins but he was a problematic source, as the very emphasis on pleasure and pain introduces for Robbins the specter of materialism and the thought that the measure of agents' "subjective" costs might be taken from the outside by the economist, or the policymaker, and not only by agents themselves. Here Wicksteed was looked to for answers. And, indeed, Wicksteed effectively purified, for Robbins, Jevons' choice into allocative choice.

Allocative choice insists that all costs are opportunity costs, that is, they consist only of the unique answer given by each chooser to the question, "what possibilities am I foreclosing when I choose, and how important are they to me?" Jevons' pleasure and pain can be cast away in favor of a model that simply posits individual scales of significance that are internally commensurable and thus responsive to price signals, and no more. That all cost is opportunity cost, which was made explicit by the Austrian economist Friedrich von Wieser, was however already implicit in the Benthamic/Jevonsian balance-driven conception of conduct. Wicksteed writes:

> We have thus arrived at the conclusion that all the heterogeneous impulses and objects of desire or aversion which appeal to any individual, whether material or spiritual, personal or communal, present or future, actual or ideal, may all be regarded as comparable with each other; for we are, as a matter of fact, constantly comparing them, weighing them against each other, and deciding which is the heaviest. And the question, "How much of this must I forgo to obtain so much of that?" is always relevant. If we are considering, for example, whether to live in the country or in the town, such different things as friendship and fresh air or fresh eggs may come into competition and comparison with each other ...[51]

Note how Wicksteed's example obscures what is at stake. His country/town alternative calls to mind less the constant comparison asserted in the first part of the quotation, which would presumably guide all conduct, and more the occasional work of a "Moral or Prudential Algebra," that is, the binary and discrete cost/benefit analysis of Benjamin Franklin's celebrated letter to Joseph Priestley from 1772.[52] Franklin's is a method for weighing the factors of a difficult life decision by putting the alternatives on either side of a ledger and striking out adjudged-equivalent pros and cons in order to see which side has value left standing. This balance contrasts with a Bentham/Jevons balance involving an indefinite range of commensurable ends and means that are continually traded off with one another and continuously guide one's conduct, in service to the best benefit yield.

Robbins, in his resistance to the monistic and directive language of utility and maximization for its utilitarian and overly rationalist implications, adopts Wicksteed's language of a genuine plurality of ends. But he does this only to completely muddle the distinction noted by Knight between economic and other approaches to ends, between one end and many, and to demonstrate that he is allied throughout with the former and not the latter approach. Robbins acknowledges in a footnote that "there is no disharmony between the conception of end here employed ... and the conception involved when it is said there is but one end of activity: the maximizing of satisfaction, 'utility,' or what not." In the note he confirms that the Wicksteed/Robbins variety of discrete "'ends,'" now tellingly put in scare quotes, "are to be regarded as proximate to the achievement of this ultimate end," that is, maximizing utility (*NS*, 15n). Once one clears away the obfuscations one sees that any more "Austrian" approach to choice in economics betrays itself as being fundamentally Jevonsian and utilitarian.[53] And, in fact, Wicksteed's choice is more Benthamic (and Austrian) than it is Jevonsian, because it does not exclude "higher" motives, but instead encompasses "all the heterogeneous impulses and objects of desire or aversion which appeal to any individual."

The modern figure most notable for his willingness to make heterogeneities commensurable and for applying the allocative choice approach to everything, the theorist of peak economic rationality, was the University of Chicago Nobelist, Gary Becker (1930–2014). Some Austrian and other heterodox thinkers on the economic Right admire Becker's defense of markets but worry about his confidence in the march of economic science, and see him as debasing human agency with his relentless utility-maximizing approach. Becker innovated thinking in crime and punishment, returning to Bentham's conception of the criminal as a rational rather than pathological actor, responding like everyone else to incentives and disincentives. His work on the allocation of time demolished the older work/leisure tradeoff, putting "leisure" in quotation marks because, in Becker's dogged emphasis on individual utility and his popularization of human capital thinking, some of what others call leisure might be thought of as productive investment, some of what others call work might be thought of as enjoyment, and so on.[54] The self-described "neo-Scholastic" economist John D. Mueller is among those who see the attention paid by earlier economists like Wicksteed and Robbins to the ends of action as somehow debased by the work of Becker and his ilk.[55] However, perhaps Becker simply had the courage of his convictions in comparison to partisans of an economic rationality that is supposed somehow to be a servant of human ends rather than their master.

Put differently and perhaps too simply, the question is this: is the microeconomic commensurability flagged here, and the allocative rationality that it allows and encourages, a function of economic agents, of economists themselves, or of specific institutions and social relations (for example the modern state, pricing markets, or the logic of capital)? Wicksteed and Robbins were humane and expansive thinkers; Wicksteed acknowledged that economic relations create pressures that produce a host of perverse and destructive effects alongside salutary ones, and Robbins did not want his work to imply that efficiency per se was a virtue. They were persuaded, however, like all theorists of the microeconomic mode, certainly not that agents are selfish hedonists, or necessarily rational, but that agents' own ends and means are in their own terms commensurable with one another: their very idea of rational decision relied on some such commensurability resulting in, or signaled by, choice. Wicksteed's text is fascinating on the ethical implications of the choice approach. He notes that even martyrdom is consistent with economic assumptions because the theory is, after all, a theory of subjective value, and martyrs simply demonstrate what they value through their apparently "incorruptible" choices. Moreover, it shouldn't puzzle the reader that a price offer for one's honor tends to elicit a resistant (as opposed to responsive or indifferent) reaction, because such an offer clarifies for the honorable that what is at stake in the proposed transaction is their honor, which it turns out they value very highly.

Wicksteed recognizes that people speak of duties as if they are in a special class apart from, and so incommensurable with, one another and with desires: "I wanted to do x," one says, "but instead I did my duty." According to him when people do so they are really just talking about things that they weigh very highly (or things that they decide they must, after due consideration, do), and when they encounter what seems to them like a conflict of duties this after all implies "that duty itself is a quantitative conception."[56] But does it really? Consider, for example, that sometimes agents find themselves in tragic situations, where however they act or refrain from acting they will necessarily do wrong. It might seem that in seeking to "minimize" wrongdoing in these circumstances agents are only acting economically. But to assimilate such a situation to cost-assessment and choice-adjustment is to misunderstand what is at stake, and might even compound the wrong. In such tragic circumstances one might need both to be aware of, and to acknowledge to oneself and others, that what one does will necessarily involve wrongdoing or other loss.[57] Robbins maintains that the economists highlight with their method the sometimes-hidden cost of every choice, and in so doing bring a kind of reality principle to those who would otherwise dream of cost-free measures. Yet, because in this scheme any one subjective cost is commensurable with any other, because consequences are not recognized in their specificity, there is no genuine loss, simply cost. In saying that the economist is a "true tragedian" Robbins plays on the reputation of the dismal science, but he has things exactly backwards. Allocative choice denies tragedy, and its economics encourages this denial. The dismal scientist is less tragedian than comedian.

In allocative choice, intra-economic-unit comparisons are assumed to be tractable, which can give false direction and hubris to economic rationality such that there is for it no such thing as a genuine dilemma. Moreover, Robbins' rigorous and effective efforts to purify economics cast aspersions on varieties of intersubjective reason, and it constrained political rationalities in particular. In the words of the philosopher Hilary Putnam, Robbins' work "persuaded the entire economics profession that *interpersonal comparisons of utility are 'meaningless.'*"[58] Ironically, despite Robbins' stated intent this feat, rather than distinguishing efficiency from virtue, only elevated it as a virtue. Efficiency as a virtue is elevated in two ways. First, in response to Robbins, "economists did not simply conclude that there was no such field as 'welfare economics.' Instead they looked (strange as this may sound) for a *value neutral criterion of optimal economic functioning.*"[59] Economists generated purified measures of welfare based on the aggregate efficiency criterion theorized by Vilfredo Pareto. "Pareto optimality" describes any of a set of allocations following which no one can be made better off without making someone else worse off. Robbins was critical of the "new welfare economics" as a putatively scientific trend,[60] pointing out in a late lecture that it too makes interpersonal utility comparisons, by assuming for example that A doesn't experience B's relative gain as a loss more profound than B's experience of gain.[61] Robbins is of course correct; economists were making an evaluation here by bracketing out of their calculations experiences like envy, when even envy should have no less status as a disutility than any other subjective cost.[62] Creative responses by Nicholas Kaldor and John Hicks, among others, might stress the importance of potential to compensate, but Robbins is right to emphasize that potential is very different from actual compensation.[63]

The problem here is that all the back and forth only reinforces faith in efficiency based in subjective value and the supposed meaninglessness or illegitimacy of utility comparisons. Yet Robbins' very examples show how we make interpersonal utility comparisons all the time, and that they are far from meaningless. Robbins certainly acknowledged this, but he refused the possibility of a rational solution. The implication of a host of choice and aggregated choice work across the spectrum, from economists who hardly recognize market failure to economists who see rampant failure, is that social rationality is grounded in the preferences of presumptively unassociated individuals and their real or ideal enactments.[64] Either the economist steps in with a (perhaps in spite of Robbins) rational solution, or refuses to step in, on behalf of a conception of efficiency thus grounded. What is declared irrational and written off, or what is short-circuited and displaced by a putatively superior (market or economic-planner) rationality, are any number of reasonable approaches to communally defined strivings, injustice, division, comparison, and conflict that are recognized by students of politics. These approaches might be inefficient from an economist's point of view, but eminently effective (or not) in bridging or resolving or realizing the issues at hand. And all of these ways of doing things in the course of their operation can have the effect of modifying the perspectives and "preferences" of participants and observers alike. They include among other things political mobilization and struggle (electoral and otherwise), legal complaints and procedures, artistic expression and reception, and more diffuse forms of publicity and even conversation. These are not social or political "choices" so much as means that parties to cooperation and conflict use to pursue ends they are trying to achieve, ends that they might or might not be in any position to trade off (for better uses of their time, etc.). The means in some cases are not separable from the ends. Such practices shouldn't be discounted by putting them, as both Robbins and many of his "new welfare" adversaries would, in an inefficient, subjective, or arbitrary, rather than a purely "scientific," so more objective and rational, basket.

Robbins also helped to elevate efficiency-as-virtue directly. By working to purify economics as a value-free science, and thus not frankly acknowledging the very virtue lodged in its name – economy – as a value, he rendered efficiency the only value left standing in a moral science with a long history of political and ethical reflection. And his insistence, along with others before and after, on the irreducibly subjective quality of costs only further made choice itself into a virtue, as a kind of signal of and for efficiency. Again, those economists persuaded, or at least spooked by and responding to, arguments against interpersonal commensurability are all committed to the reality or heuristic or rational standard of intra-personal commensurability. Not allowed to judge in any a priori way whether diseconomy is really going on, because each individual works with their own inscrutable criteria, subjective-value economists are like Max Weber's Protestant saints, eager for signs of salvation, even while knowing that the mind of God is unknowable. They say when one makes a choice, one is signaling what one values. For modern economics, choice is that divine sign, as suggested by the quasi-theological, but now standard, language of "revealed preference."[65]

Economics and expertise

As a matter of fact it is difficult for Robbins, or anyone working in the microeconomic mode, to think of decision-making in terms other than choice. Surprisingly deep into the essay, Robbins acknowledges that the market economic relations he and other economists mainly study require non-market institutional frameworks – laws, courts, etc. – that are what other economists call "public goods," that is, in Robbins' phrasing "not capable of being elicited by price bids" (*NS*, 144). Yet for him, as for legions of postwar "social choice" and "public choice" economists in the US and elsewhere, these frameworks are themselves the product of choice. And so political decisions are understood in this tradition in relation to aggregates of political preferences, and then, because of the indeterminacy of such aggregations, suspected of being arbitrary, and so in some hands thought to be ideally limited to producing those goods that can be shown to be rationally choice-worthy by all.[66] Robbins (and others) would never think of political choices as following from economic science, but by reducing politics to a matter of individual choice and its aggregates he participates in "the disenchantment of politics by economics."[67] And, because individual choices are thought of in terms of price bids and responses to them, real or ideal markets that equili-brate choices read as signs of economy become, on the very narrow criteria of choice-rationality and even, as it were, in the breach, the very model of rational institutions. Here, various judgments by which even well-functioning markets are deemed irrational – for example, in the perversity of many of their distributions of rewards – can be sidelined as ethical and thus, on this account, irreducibly "subjective" concerns.

Robbins knows he cannot entirely escape the normativity lodged in his discipline, and thus at the end of the essay he wrestles with the meaning of rationality in economics. He acknowledges that this rationality is, essentially, efficiency or economy, and that the "criterion of economy which follows from our original definitions is the securing of given ends with least means." Economic rationality seems then to be instrumental; it seems to serve given ends: "there are," Robbins repeats, "no economic ends. There are only economical and uneconomical ways of achieving given ends" (*NS*, 145). Economic rationality appears to echo Hume's notoriously thin notion of reason, that reason is the "slave of the passions," and that "'Tis not contrary to reason to prefer the destruction of the whole world to the scratching of my finger." But Humean reason is not the same as economic rationality. Hume adds that it is "as little contrary to reason to prefer even my own acknowledg'd lesser good to my greater, and have a more ardent affection for the former than for the latter."[68] There is nothing irrational, in Hume's sense, about pure diseconomy or waste as adjudged by the waster. Thus Hume takes us far from Robbins, and from a science that, as many other economists can and have explicitly acknowledged, "is built on welfare foundations."[69]

The pursuit of economy or efficiency does not leave ends untouched. Robbins' concluding remarks on economic rationality in relation to harmony and consistency unwittingly betray rationality's ethical and political status. On his view, scientific economics helps us choose rationally, and choosing rationally "is nothing more and nothing less than choice with complete awareness of the alternatives rejected." Economics enhances our perception in a way that "makes it possible for us to select a system of ends which are mutually consistent with one another" (*NS*, 152), and it is this very consistency, this relative harmonization of ends, that rationality consists in. Robbins concludes the essay with a peroration that can embrace both today's textbook rationalists and their behavioral critics. Economics, he writes:

> relies upon no assumption that individuals will always act rationally. But it does depend for its practical *raison d'être* upon the assumption that it is desirable that they should do so. It does assume that, within the bounds of necessity, it is desirable to choose ends which can be achieved harmoniously.
> ... Economics does depend, if not for its existence, at least for its significance, on an ultimate valuation – the

affirmation that rationality and ability to choose with knowledge is desirable.

Economics is "that branch of knowledge which, above all others, is the symbol and safeguard of rationality in social arrangements" (*NS*, 157–158).

Note the slippage from economists as humble servants of the public to something else: guardians at least, if not masters. This slippage calls attention to what a peculiar form of expertise modern economics is. The question of the place of expertise in politics is a very old one. Well over two millennia ago Plato attacked democracy on the basis of its lack of expertise. Would you take a poll or a vote to figure out what to do if you were ill? Of course not. You would consult a physician, someone with the requisite virtue, with the specific expertise to make you better, rather than consult the majority demos who, according to Plato, have no ability to make you better or worse, because they are ignorant. In the *Republic* Plato argues, notoriously, that on this basis the people are entirely unfit to rule; he substitutes his virtuous guardians in their place.

In his *Protagoras*, however, we learn about the perspective of a defender of Plato's democratic city, Athens (the dialogue is set during its so-called Golden Age, soon before the ruinous Peloponnesian War). The title character Protagoras, when asked about Athenian attitudes toward virtue, defends a general expertise of the city that is both taught and learned by all through daily interactions: the civic virtue that qualifies the people to rule. The presence and exercise of civic virtue doesn't mean that more specialized virtues go unrecognized and unappreciated; on the contrary, they are essential. But they are essential for technical as opposed to practical matters. Which is to say, in Robbins' terms, that specific virtues are essential for figuring out the means to given ends, not for the determination of ends. According to Plato's dialogue, if Athens decided to build something then they would consult builders for advice about how to do it, and won't listen to others if they are not builders. But if it's a question of whether and what to build, or any "general decision on how our city should be run," then builders don't have any more say than anyone else. Then "anyone at all can get up and give an opinion ... he could be rich or poor, an aristocrat or a nobody."[70] The question of whether or what to build is a practical question, a question of ends, and not a technical question, and the people at large are fully competent to address it.

Such is the spirit of Robbins' conclusion on the significance of economic science, but it is necessarily violated by the letter: as the "safeguard of rationality in social arrangements" economics outs itself as a self-styled all-purpose expertise. On this understanding, economists are always useful no matter what is at stake, and not to consult them always poses a danger. And this perfectly suits the position economics has assumed across the globe as the predominant policy science. Robbins is hostile to any understanding of economics proper as policy science; he agrees with other disciplinary critics that science doesn't "read off" into policy. But Robbins, like other critics, misunderstands such reading off as an unwarranted overstretching of economic knowledge, or as the imposition of the subjective values or biases of individual scientists, or both at the same time. These are red herrings. Robbins' own understanding of choice and rationality suggests instead a tendency built deep into the grammar of the discipline.

The vast majority of contemporary economists, along with their fellow citizens, now understand themselves to be living in an "economy" that, by definition, requires expert guidance and management. Those in the discipline who decry this understanding as social engineering are unable consistently to eschew a version of what they name.[71] On the contrary, echoing the counterrevolutionary Enlightenment bent of their political-economic forebears, the critics of social engineering themselves articulate the existence of a field, a field of microeconomic choice, whose patterns they have the expertise to understand and in which others are improperly meddling. This is the mode, for example, of the US Cato Institute, a self-described "libertarian" policy think-tank. Speaking on behalf of a social field and its laws they and other critics of social engineering prescribe their own "portfolio of projects,"[72] even as these are seen by them as "corrective" or "deregulatory" measures. If Paul Samuelson, Gregory Mankiw, and other mainstream Fordist or post-Fordist textbook writers are in their greater or lesser attentiveness to market failure named social engineers, then their critics are skeptical engineers, squaring off against their more seemingly activist colleagues and other meddlers as guardians themselves of Robbins' "rationality in social arrangements."[73] The logic of the microeconomic mode is a governmental one. Political economy once promoted individual independence and democratic reform; economics now promotes "better choices" and expert systems management.

Governing interest

To understand how a science based on economic rationality builds a non-ethical ethics and antipolitical politics one final feature of Robbins' essay deserves a closer look. This feature sees political conflict as stemming from the interior of the choosing self in a way that opens that self to therapeutic examination and control, in part by turning focus away from matters connecting or dividing individuals and groups. Robbins' essay notoriously considers differences over ends as leading only either to "thy blood or mine" violence or "live and let live" liberal tolerance, as if these differences don't develop out of and inform relations with others and are not amenable to alternative resolutions (*NS*, 150). More politically fateful, though, is Robbins' way of theoretically resolving such differences in advance, his peculiar insistence that the conflicts of interest that animate political life aren't what they appear to be. Here the approach economics takes to producing more harmonious conduct, the turn inward for the self or other economic unit, comes to the fore.

Robbins writes: "It may well be that there may exist differences as regards ultimate ends in modern society which render some conflict inevitable. But it is clear that many of our most pressing difficulties arise ... because our aims are not co-ordinated" (*NS*, 156). The aims that are not coordinated here are not the aims of opposed factions or interest groups, for example the interests of debtors versus those of creditors, as in the political theory of James Madison.[74] Robbins makes such oppositions look more apparent than real by grounding them in the opposed aims of individuals. For example, he notes, many individuals are at one and the same time consumers seeking cheapness and workers seeking security. Thus, "(e)verywhere our difficulties seem to arise, not so much from divisions between the different members of the body politic, as from, as it were, split personalities on the part of each one of them" (*NS*, 156). This is a remarkable and consequential claim, one that Knight picked up on in his review: "I am rather surprised to read … that the difficulties of society arise more from intellectual confusions in the minds of individuals than from conflicts of interests."[75] If it seems bizarre to think of social problems as resulting from individuals' intellectual confusions, this is if anything an increasingly prevalent view among social scientists. Behavioral economists and political psychologists frequently point to such confusions as feeders of twenty-first-century crises, and of political outcomes – like Brexit and the election of Trump – that strike these scientists as irrational.

If our problems are more about individual confusion than about anything else, then they are amenable to therapeutic solutions rather than political ones: to self-help and adjustment to the way things are, rather than to collective transformation of common circumstances. And the implications run further. Economics is the discipline uniquely suited to dissolve now-deemed-irrational group attachments that purport to advance common interests (of class, region, what have you). Economics shows, according to Robbins, how individuals' plural involvements are readily resolved into possibly clashing preferences within them. Thus the therapeutic solution is itself a transformative politics, but in disguise. The passage on split personalities is marked by a footnote referencing texts that re-theorize sovereignty (*NS* 156n), texts from Robbins' early pluralist education, an education that coincided with his youthful guild socialism.[76] By reducing pluralists' appreciation of individuals' multiple involvements in different associations to multiple aims within selves, Robbins effectively turns his teachers' insights on their head. If Harold Laski and other critics of the modern state had intended to deconstruct the idea of a unitary sovereignty, then Robbins' microeconomic approach essentially reconstructs its monistic rule.

Economics re-founds sovereignty firstly at the level of a choosing unit that ultimately has only one interest, one that a psycho-economic science of "thinking slow" might help any chooser sort out: this is the Bentham/Jevons "balance" that should, whether it does or not, inform choice.[77] And economics re-founds sovereignty secondly at the level of an administrative order that can better "harmonize" the activities of choosing units with the aid of a managerial-economic science of incentives and disincentives. Whether this latter economic sovereignty takes the form of regulation or deregulation is beside the point. Either way, its ruling performances aim to better govern subjects through interests that are never untouched but are in fact re-formed by government, as every new measure introduces incentives or disincentives that effectively change the balance of one's rational choice.

Robbins of course intends none of these consequences. He wants to free economics proper as much as possible from psychology, and as much as possible from policy. However, the point here is that intentions, biases, etc. are not what is at issue but instead the more foundational logic of economic rationality itself. Economic rationality displaces political sovereignty with economic sovereignty. Thus the political significance of economic rationality is that through this displacement struggles against domination or any other form of conflict and cooperation over shared space are reframed: they are reframed as problems of domestic and social admin-istration, problems, in Robbins' terms, of more harmonious government. In this way, the logic of more-or-less rational allocative choice limits political understanding and strait-jackets collective action. Such constraints are convenient for dominant classes and interests, but they are particularly ill-suited to the scale and character of multiple contemporary crises. The attempt to address these crises through economic government necessarily falls short, and it engenders more of the problems that economic rationality is so ill-suited to solve.

5
Conclusion

The political theory of economic rationality has helped to build a world where it is possible and perhaps even prudent to think like Gary Becker. Becker takes the subjective-value allocative choice tradition to its logical conclusions. Here's Becker in 1976:

> Good health and a long life are important aims of most persons, but ... somewhat better health or a longer life may be sacrificed because they conflict with other aims ... Therefore, a person may be a heavy smoker or so committed to work as to omit all exercise, not necessarily because he is ignorant of the consequences or "incapable" of using the information he possesses, but because the lifespan forfeited is not worth the cost to him of quitting smoking or working less intensively ...
>
> According to the economic approach, therefore, *most* (if not all!) deaths are to some extent "suicides" in the sense that they could have been postponed if more resources had been invested in prolonging life.[1]

The passage is remarkable for a number of reasons, and one can't help but think its hubristic rationalism might have single-handedly inspired a behavioral backlash in the discipline. But we live in a world in which many students, workers, and consumers can reasonably see themselves as investors of sorts, continuously calculating payoffs from their choices, for example of what to learn. Becker's passage speaks of and to a world so permeated by social and machine technologies of commensurability and choice that such an orientation is possible, even making sense to those with comparatively little to bring to market, and making even more sense almost fifty years later with the rise of the internet and the explosion of consumer finance.

Becker was no doubt insensitive (the passage rankles) but he wasn't at all ignorant. He must have been at least somewhat aware of the history of suicide in philosophical reflection, of its central place in individualist traditions that center something like choice. Stoicism and existentialism, for all their differences, reflect on suicide in somewhat similar terms, for what they see as its intimate connection to freedom. But for Becker most death is suicide, and its timing is made commensurable with a broad range of action and inaction reframed as risks and hedges. Thus what at first suggests radical freedom (it's all up to you and your budgeting) looks more like its opposite. It's no longer even clear what suicide is (thus the tell-tale quotation marks), just as it's no longer clear what leisure is, or what a household is as opposed to a firm: any number of distinctions are deliberately and provocatively obliterated by Becker's approach. It's never even clear in Becker's work how what Jeremy Bentham called the "political sanction," that is, legal prohibition, is qualitatively different (as somehow distinctively coercive) from any other price when it does, after all, present a choice (obey or be punished X amount). Behavioralists in their reaction to Becker have done a great service with their reminder that economists' choices exist within choice architectures: they are always already governed. Economics as politics and political theory buttresses and, in its disavowal of politics, shrouds this government. The shroud is removed by the new management- and psychology-affirming economists, even as they serve the same masters.

If it seems strange to think that your health and very longevity are up to you – where everything is converted to risk and so somehow predispositions or vulnerabilities are all assessed, accidents are not really accidents, contingencies not really contingencies, and a world of animate and inanimate others is thoroughly mastered – it's really not any more absurd than the messages of responsibilization that have been everywhere for a while now (from diet to exercise to personal security, etc., they're all on and up to you). At least they had been everywhere, until more recently in conjunction with the behavioral backlash some are being displaced by messages of de-responsibilization, messages about vulnerability to one's own affect, vulnerability to algorithms, etc. Although these latter might seem to reintroduce a world of constitutive relations, they are actually the flip side of the Becker view. One is either sovereign or helpless. If anything is needed it is either better self-management, which is another prudent investment for the rational agent, or better systems management, which is a matter of expertly guided monetary policy and fiscal policy (skewed to the few) and policing and behavioral nudging (skewed to the many). Other modes of politics are mostly ruled out or suspect, called rent-seeking, according to the political theory of economic rationality.

The aim here is not to substitute an invented, quasi- or pseudo-Aristotelian *"Homo politicus"* for *"Homo economicus."*[2] For one thing, to think that Becker's view, or that of his behavioral opponents, is merely or even mostly a misunderstanding is itself a misunderstanding.[3] Instead it is a mode of rule, one that fits hand in glove with existing systems of domination, leaving them entirely untouched. For another thing, if a big problem is the inadequacy of economic rationality to address as opposed to exacerbate existing problems, then the alternative is not to provide any ready-made solution. That would simply extend the politics-by-other means logic of the political theory of economics, as illustrated, for example, by the choices of philanthropic billionaires.[4] But it is worth remembering that some of the same institutions that were built by egalitarian reformers in the attack on the aristocracies of the eighteenth and nineteenth centuries have unknown potential today. Just as no one knows the future, no one knows the extent to which institutions can contain or redirect economic rationality; witness the understandable confusion and dissensus among economists, not to mention others, about the limits of unprecedented recent central bank maneuvers. What is called "the state" is not one but many things, and one of their potentials is the ability to channel public power to public purpose. This obvious fact, that the state is a field of struggle with uncertain boundaries and that it has served not only domination but freedom, in part by opposing multiple "private" forms of rule, is worth recalling. Not so long ago even Milton Friedman could briefly nod to the legitimacy of democratic power and purpose, by acknowledging that the state doesn't just threaten or secure freedom, but is "an instrument through which we can exercise our freedom."[5]

As many critics have argued, microeconomics is limited even in how it characterizes the field of market activities themselves. After all, once one understands what an "externality" is, it doesn't take much to realize that every market transaction involves these, that one could think of any field of iterative practice that one would call an "economy" as itself a cumulative externality.[6] All one needs to do is take seriously Karl Polanyi's distinction and adopt a substantive rather than formal view of a transaction, and one can recognize that the relations that it is dependent on, and the effects whether positive or negative it has on those relations, are not party to the transaction and so not priced. All the more reason, then, to take seriously the question of institutions and institutional renewal or transformation, because the relations we call institutional are congelations of power. This has been well understood by self-consciously political economists in the subjective value mode, who succeeded over the years in weakening some institutions and strengthening others that have had the effect of empowering transnational actors, insulating them from democratic pressure.[7] And, although there is certainly good reason to think of these actors' power as that of an organized class, a more disturbing possibility is that of the sometimes disorganized preeminence of individuals with unfathomable wealth and often multiple citizenships (many citizenships, and not only in poorer jurisdictions, are available for a price). Several of these individuals seem through their actions and rhetoric to be pushing the logic of the microeconomic mode to new limits in attempting to escape from messes they help make: whether through new forms of life-extending body fashioning, or pre-purchased climate apocalypse New Zealand estates, or the ultimate exit dream of space colonization.

The limits of the politics of the microeconomic mode are apparent everywhere. Yes, economists working in this mode have successfully designed some of the most humane responses to the 2020 pandemic, but the adoption and success of their plans, like those of the more successful public health agencies, has required effective state actors working amid relatively high levels of trust and solidarity. Ever aware of the importance of the latter, some US public intellectuals are calling more attention to the limitations of any perspective that begins, as economic rationality does, with preference and choice. Allocative choice and the moralizing that is supplemental to it are a dead end; instead, begin with what gathers the differently minded together, begin with what calls for action. And so on the Right, Yuval Levin has emphasized the requisites of trust and solidarity. The key for people to be more effective and to rebuild institutional power is to stop asking themselves what they want or what they should do in some abstract sense. They could instead be aware when acting of their institutional locale, and "We each have to say, given my role here, what's my responsibility?"[8] Similarly, on the Left, Keeanga-Yamahtta Taylor has attacked some of the subject-centered discourses circulating in contemporary social movements. And this might speak to broad confusion about what institutions and roles actually are, as some, in their Beckerian solipsism, might mistake their self-identification as "white ally" for an institutional role. "I just think this whole ally thing ... has to go," Taylor says. Why? "Because it makes it seem like, well, over here in our America, everything is great – we just need to improve your America ... No! Have you looked at what's happening in their America? ... The life expectancy of ordinary white men and women has gone into reverse." Taylor follows with an analysis of racism as a special burden for some but as problem for the republic as a whole, its bipartisan deployment over the years having successfully undermined public provision. What's left is a country riddled with injustice and completely ill-prepared to weather the storms of the pandemic.[9]

All this is a reminder of our starting point. Economic rationality is only apparently instrumental; it channels action with little if any regard to what is called for. Political struggles for justice or advantage are more genuinely instrumental than economic rationality, in the sense that their focus is effectiveness. Economic rationality is always ready to sacrifice effectiveness on the altar of efficiency and yield, as evidenced by the recent cult of "disruptive innovation," an old idea in competitive capitalism, certainly, but taken to new heights by agents and agencies with shockingly short time horizons, "fixing" what sometimes isn't at all broken. The question for any politics that would at least tame modalities of economic rationality, is, "how to get to result X?" Here the ends are inseparable from the means, as shoring up the group or institutional power needed to get to X might require extensive organizing across differences, negotiating, coalition-building, and other steps before any, or as part of any, engagement or confrontation with one's adversaries. The instrumentalism of this politics, involving as it does plurality, is always more-than-instrumental. It is not conceivable without a measure of communicative action and other ends and means that might seem foreign to instrumentality but that are absolutely essential to the accomplishment of the political goals, goals that require building the power that they rely on for their realization. Ordinary prudence, as Adam Smith, and Machiavelli among others before him, understood, is inadequate to this politics; it requires something like the "superior prudence" that earns Smith's admiration in the revised *Theory of Moral Sentiments*, published during a time of political revolution. As in 1789, today's aristocrats aren't by any means the source of all of our difficulties. Yet they consistently stand in the way of attempts to call people's sustained attention to those difficulties: to break through the new kinds of collective action problems that have been generated, in part, by the effective institutionalization of politics in the microeconomic mode. If mainstream political scientists are starting to give a persistent political problem a name – oligarchy[10] – then surely others can take up the charge to organize against it.

Notes

1 Introduction

1 Lionel Robbins, *An Essay on the Nature and Significance of Economic Science*, 3rd edn. (New York: New York University Press, 1984 [1932, 1935]), 16.

2 Karl Polanyi, referencing formal as opposed to substantive economics in "The Economy as Instituted Process," in K. Polanyi, C. M. Arensberg, and H. W. Pearson, eds., *Trade and Market in the Early Empires: Economies in History and Theory* (New York: The Free Press, 1957), 243.

3 This basic framework for rationality can accommodate not only for any number of metrics of cost or benefit applied by the choosing unit; it can account for and contend with all manner of supplemental conditions: technical, including informational, constraints plus other departures from any frictionless account of rational choice.

4 See, for example, Frank H. Knight, "The Nature of Economic Science in Some Recent Discussion," *American Economic Review* 24:2 (1934), 236 and passim.

5 I borrow this application of the Weberian language of disenchantment from William Davies, *The Limits of Neoliberalism: Authority, Sovereignty, and the Logic of Competition* (London: Sage Publications, 2014), 1–34.

6 Karl Marx, *Capital: A Critique of Political Economy, Volume One*, trans. Ben Fowkes (London: Penguin Books, 1976 [1867]), 254.

7 Karl Polanyi, *The Great Transformation: The Political and Economic Origins of our Time* (Boston: Beacon Press, 1957 [1944]).

8 For a now-canonical modern statement of this ancient concern see Amartya K. Sen, "Rational Fools: A Critique of the Behavioral Foundations of Economic Theory," *Philosophy and Public Affairs* 6:4 (1977), 317–344.

9 I borrow this language from Jane Elliott, *The Microeconomic Mode: Political Subjectivity in Contemporary Popular Aesthetics* (New York: Columbia University Press, 2018).

10 What economists do has arguably departed substantially from what they teach; David Colander, "What Economists Teach and What Economists Do," *Journal of Economic Education* 36:3 (2005), 249–260.

11 It should be said that the "best-selling" claim regarding Gregory Mankiw's *Principles* (see Chapter 2, below) is hard to verify, but the text remains very much representative. For a promising departure from the usual introduction to the discipline, one that begins not with allocative choice but with "the capitalist revolution," see the Curriculum Open-Access Resources in Economics (CORE) project at https://www.core-econ.org/the-economy/book/text/01.html.

2 Textbook Rationality and the Behavioral Critique

1 Jean-Baptiste Say, *A Treatise on Political Economy, or the Production, Distribution, and Consumption of Wealth*, 4th edn., trans. C. R. Prinsep (Philadelphia: Lippincott, 1850), xlv, vi.

2 Michael Parkin, *Microeconomics*, global edn., 2016 (emphasis in original), quoted in Jane Elliott, *The Microeconomic Mode: Political Subjectivity in Contemporary Popular Aesthetics* (New York: Columbia University Press, 2018), 188n. Elliott's work of literary criticism has helped inspire me in my approach to the textbook view to emphasize the figure of allocative choice and the rhetorical mapping it does.

3 Paul Samuelson, *Economics* (New York: McGraw-Hill Inc., 1976), 3 (emphasis in original).

4 Courtney Weaver, "Inside the Weird World of Cryonics," *The Financial Times*, December 18, 2015. https://www.ft.com/content/d634e198-a435-11e5-873f-68411a84f346.

5 See, for example, "The Invisible Paw," Freakonomics Radio, April 4, 2018. http://freakonomics.com/podcast/animal-economics/.

6   Gregory Mankiw, *Principles of Economics*, 9th edn. (Boston: Cengage Learning, 2021), 4 (emphasis in original).
7   Ibid., 2.
8   Ibid., 3.
9   Ibid., 4.
10 Ibid.
11 Ibid., 5–6.
12 We might on occasion set up our own incentives, to help for instance in keeping a commitment (think of Odysseus and the Sirens or stickk.com), even as we often do that by involving others (here one's sailors or fellow netizens). And keep in mind that economists' incentives aren't always about market prices, but could involve other sorts of prices (for example, loss of reputation).
13 Friedrich Hayek, "Use of Knowledge in Society," *American Economic Review* 35:4 (1945), 519–530.
14 Mankiw, *Principles of Economics*, 14.
15 Ibid., 5–6.
16 Jacques Le Goff, *Time, Work, and Culture in the Middle Ages*, trans. A. Goldhammer (Chicago: University of Chicago Press, 1982); David S. Landes, *Revolution in Time: Clocks and the Making of the Modern World* (Cambridge, MA: Harvard University Press, 1983).
17 Mankiw, *Principles of Economics*, 7–13.
18 Ibid., 709–710. Compare Adam Tooze, *Crashed: How a Decade of Financial Crises Changed the World* (New York: Viking, 2018). Mankiw did integrate new discussions of bank capital and leverage as a result of the crash; see Gregory Mankiw, "Reflections of a Textbook Author" (2019), 11. https://scholar.harvard.edu/files/mankiw/files/reflections_of_a_textbook_author.pdf. Although dated 2021, the 9th edn. of *Principles of Economics* went to press before the 2020 pandemic.
19 For a useful overview of authors and perspectives see Malcolm Rutherford, "Institutional Economics: Then and Now," *Journal of Economic Perspectives* 15:3 (2001), 173–194.
20 John Maynard Keynes, *The General Theory of Employment, Interest, and Money* (New York: Harvest/HBJ, 1964), Preface and Book I: Introduction, v–34. Writing in the mid-1930s, Keynes simply called the economics he criticized "the classical theory" ("neoclassical" was only coined some ten years earlier). Often, because of its reference to "animal spirits," Keynes's approach is read as a forerunner to behavioral economics. But if that means characterizing economic actors as irrational this is

largely a misreading. Keynes instead revives the "general glut" specter of Robert Malthus and Karl Marx, offering analysis of a collective action problem of collapsing effective demand, complicated by structural class differences generally unrecognized in the postclassical mainstream.

21 "Macroeconomics" was the linguistic predecessor and spur to the coinage of "microeconomics."

22 "Neoliberal" and "neoliberalism" are contested terms that have inspired a rich literature in several disciplines. My relatively broad use here follows William Davies' interest in a disenchanted politics from Davies, *The Limits of Neoliberalism* (London: Sage Publications, 2014).

23 Mankiw, *Principles of Economics*, 453.

24 If not in our sense of corruption, public choice definitely assumes corruption from a classical political-theoretical perspective, as understood for example by Niccolò Machiavelli in his *Discourses*. The political actor on a public choice account doesn't recognize politics as a field evaluatively distinct from the economic. Corruption in this classical sense mustn't be confused with moral badness; on this view, if the office-holder were moral or altruistic in their self-interest it would be no less corrupting of republican institutions.

25 For a narrative and critique of this evolution focusing on the university department supposedly most devoted to free markets see David Colander and Craig Freedman, *Where Economics Went Wrong: Chicago's Abandonment of Classical Liberalism* (Princeton: Princeton University Press, 2019). But more is going on here than an overstepping lack of restraint among scientists: "the problem of neo-liberalism was not how to cut out or contrive a free space of the market within an already given political society, as in the liberalism of Adam Smith and the eighteenth century. The problem of neo-liberalism is rather how the overall exercise of political power can be modeled on the principles of a market economy." Michel Foucault, *The Birth of Biopolitics: Lectures at the Collège de France, 1978–1979*, trans. G. Burchell (Basingstoke: Palgrave Macmillan, 2008), 131.

26 Samuelson, *Economics*, 7 (emphasis in original).

27 G. K. Chesterton, *What's Wrong With the World* (1910), quoted in Georges Canguilhem, *The Normal and the Pathological*, trans. Carolyn R. Fawcett (New York: Zone Books, 1991), 258.

28 Mankiw, *Principles of Economics*, 25–26 (emphasis in original).

29 Ibid., 4.

30 Samuelson, *Economics*, 806–810.

31 See the Royal Swedish Academy of Science's press release of 13 October 1992, https://www.nobelprize.org/prizes/economic-sciences/1992/ceremony-speech/.

32 Philip Wicksteed, *The Common Sense of Political Economy* (London: Macmillan & Co., 1910), 3 and 21.

33 Mankiw, *Principles of Economics*, 428, 430. The prolific Nobel-prize winner Amartya Sen, a critic of standard accounts of economic rationality from within the discipline, attacks the textbook equation between optimizing and maximizing behavior along with other conflations within and exclusions from models of rational choice. See, for example, Sen, "Maximization and the Act of Choice," *Econometrica* 65:4 (1997), 745–779.

34 Anthony Laden, "Keep on Keeping On: The Structure and Significance of Ongoing Actions," unpublished paper. See also Laden, *Reasoning: A Social Picture* (Oxford: Oxford University Press), 24–31, for the distinction as applied to the activity of reasoning.

35 Adam Smith, *An Inquiry into the Nature and Causes of the Wealth of Nations*, eds. R. H. Campbell and A. S. Skinner (Indianapolis: Liberty Fund, 1981), vol. I, 265–267 and passim.

36 Mankiw, *Principles of Economics*, 419–442.

37 Ibid., 430.

38 Ibid., 443.

39 Ibid., 447–466.

40 Ibid., 458.

41 Milton Friedman, "The Methodology of Positive Economics," in Friedman, *Essays in Positive Economics* (Chicago: University of Chicago Press, 1953), 3–43.

42 See especially Herbert A. Simon, *Administrative Behavior*, 4th edn. (New York: The Free Press, 1997), and Simon, "A Behavioral Model of Rational Choice," *The Quarterly Journal of Economics* 69:1 (1955), 99–118.

43 Herbert A. Simon, "Rational Decision-Making in Business Organizations," Prize Lecture (1978). https://www.nobelprize.org/prizes/economic-sciences/1978/simon/lecture/.

44 Herbert A. Simon, "Human Nature in Politics: The Dialogue of Psychology with Political Science," *American Political Science Review* 79:2 (1985), 297.

45 Herbert A. Simon, "Decision-Making: Rational, Nonrational, and Irrational," *Educational Administration Quarterly* 29:3 (1993), 395.

46 For these and other examples see Richard H. Thaler, *Misbehaving* (New York: W. W. Norton and Co., 2015).

47 Versions of the story have been told, for example by Albert O. Hirschman in *The Passions and the Interests: Arguments for Capitalism Before Its Triumph* (Princeton: Princeton University Press, 1977).

48 Richard H. Thaler, "From Cashews to Nudges: The Evolution of Behavioral Economics," Prize Lecture (2017), 491. See https://www.nobelprize.org/uploads/2018/01/thaler-lecture.pdf.

49 The other attributed causes as stated are similarly individual: "Greed and corruption helped to create the crisis, but simple human frailty played a key role," Richard H. Thaler and Cass R. Sunstein, *Nudge: Improving Decisions About Health, Wealth, and Happiness*, revised and expanded edition (New York: Penguin, 2009), 271. This afterword to the second edition is gone from the third.

50 The psychological literature on democratic incompetence is substantial, and often capable of generating headlines: "Human brains aren't built for self-rule, says Shawn Rosenberg. That's more evident than ever." https://www.politico.com/magazine/story/2019/09/08/shawn-rosenberg-democracy-228045. For a more serious and scholarly treatment influenced by political-psychological research in addition to traditional survey data, see Christopher H. Achen and Larry M. Bartels, *Democracy for Realists* (Princeton: Princeton University Press, 2017).

51 Richard H. Thaler and Cass R. Sunstein, *Nudge: The Final Edition* (New York: Penguin, 2021).

52 Ibid., 127.

53 William Maurer on *Hidden Brain*, "Emotional Currency: How Money Shapes Human Relationships," January 13, 2020. https://www.npr.org/transcripts/795246685.

54 For an original and compelling account of the origins and fate of transaction-cost thinking in economics, from a critique of the discipline's fundamental assumptions in light of the existence and growth of firms to a perverse yet coherent and highly influential re-description of firms' meaning and function, see Abraham Singer, *The Form of the Firm* (Oxford: Oxford University Press, 2019), chs. 3–6 (52–114).

55 Joel Waldfogel, "The Deadweight Loss of Christmas," *American Economic Review* 83:5 (1993), 1328–1336.

56 Thaler, *Misbehaving*, 132–139.

57 Mankiw, *Principles of Economics*, 5, quoting Steven E. Landsburg, *The Armchair Economist: Economics and Everyday Life*.

3 Political Economy

1 Gregory Mankiw, *Principles of Economics*, 9th edn. (Boston: Cengage, 2021), 8, quoting Adam Smith, *An Inquiry into the Nature and Causes of the Wealth of Nations*, R. H. Campbell, A. S. Skinner, and W. B. Todd, eds. (Indianapolis: Liberty Fund reprint, 1981 [1776]), I.ii.2, 26–27; hereafter referred to in text as "*WN*." My discussion of this passage and related material is indebted to Samuel Fleischacker's writing and teaching; see especially Fleischacker, "Talking to My Butcher: Self-Interest, Exchange, and Freedom in the *Wealth of Nations*," in Paul Sagar, ed., *Interpreting Adam Smith: Critical Essays* (Cambridge: Cambridge University Press, forthcoming). This is not to say that Fleischacker's reading necessarily supports my more political rendering.

2 Richard H. Thaler and Cass R. Sunstein, *Nudge: Improving Decisions About Health, Wealth, and Happiness*, revised and expanded edition (New York: Penguin, 2009), 271.

3 Paul Krugman, "How Did Economists Get it so Wrong?," *New York Times Magazine*, September 2, 2009.

4 The range of recognized policy expertise can get very narrow indeed. Notoriously, US President Barack Obama's 2009 crisis team was dominated by figures with close ties to Wall Street, and the only non-economist was then-New York Federal Reserve head Timothy Geithner (appointed by Obama to lead Treasury, now heading a private equity firm). There were, for example, no securities lawyers or historians of finance in the daily meetings, two of a few other groups of specialists who might have offered substantial relevant expertise for the crisis at hand.

5 On voice and exit see Albert O. Hirschman, *Exit Voice and Loyalty: Responses to Decline in Firms, Organizations, and States* (Cambridge, MA: Harvard University Press, 1970).

6 Milton Friedman, *Capitalism and Freedom* (Chicago: University of Chicago Press, 1962), 3. Many political scientists by contrast lament the effects of inter-city competition, particularly competition for investment capital, on urban government and urban life. Interestingly, in this earlier work Friedman hadn't entirely let go of an anomalous Aristotelian sentiment. In a passage preceding the one on local government he writes that government is not only "necessary to preserve our freedom, it is an instrument through which we can exercise our freedom" (2).

This civic humanist moment is gone by *Free to Choose*, which credits intervening "public choice" work as an influence.

7 Milton Friedman and Rose Friedman, *Free to Choose: A Personal Statement* (New York: Harcourt Brace Jovanovich, 1980), 13–24. The Friedmans state that it was Smith himself who "gave us the answer [to the mysteries of market coordination] 200 years ago," 13.

8 Ibid., ix–x.

9 "The field of *political economy* (sometimes called the field of *public choice*) uses the methods of economics to study how government works." Mankiw, *Principles of Economics*, 9th edn. (Boston: Cengage, 2021), 453 (emphasis in original).

10 Elizabeth Popp Berman, *Thinking like an Economist* (Princeton: Princeton University Press, 2022).

11 "Each tradesman or artificer derives his subsistence from the employment not of one, but of a hundred or a thousand different customers. Though in some measure obliged to all, therefore, he is not absolutely dependent upon any one of them" (*WN* III.iv.12, 420).

12 Alfred Marshall, *Principles of Economics* (London: Macmillan & Co., 1890), 58–59. Marshall thought that Bentham "wrote little on economics himself." The extent of Bentham's work in the field wasn't widely known until Werner Stark's three-volume twentieth-century collection, and is only now coming fully into view with two published and three forthcoming volumes edited by Michael Quinn. Although Bentham's work on political economy contains some strikingly modern insights (for example, his justifications for licenses and patents and more general understanding of property as expectation, and in glimpses of the multiplier and some development of a credit understanding of money before pulling back to a more conventional view), it is for the most part Smithian in outlook. Bentham himself distinguishes his project from Smith's ("His object was the science: my object is the art") at the beginning of *Manual of Political Economy*; Jeremy Bentham, *Writings on Political Economy, Volume I, Collected Works of Jeremy Bentham* (hereafter [CW]), ed. M. Quinn (Oxford: Oxford University Press, 2016), 168.

13 There are many examples scattered throughout Bentham's political economy and other "policy" writings of both epistemic and motivational advantages to individual over state action. "Government in general is unfit for the exercise of a lucrative occupation in comparison of individuals ... [It lacks] personal

interest, that indispensable whetstone to ingenuity and spur to vigilance." Jeremy Bentham, *The Collected Works of Jeremy Bentham: Writings on Political Economy, Volume II* (CW), ed. M. Quinn (Oxford: Oxford University Press, 2019), 168. Hayek was much more aware than Marshall of Bentham's political economy, which no doubt shaped his own economics and knowledge work that he thought was "his most original contribution to economics." He reports: "I discovered in studying the papers of Jeremy Bentham at University College [where he started the first Bentham Committee] that Bentham had been a very good economist." Friedrich Hayek, *Hayek on Hayek: An Autobiographical Dialogue*, S. Kresge and L. Wenar, eds. (Chicago: University of Chicago Press, 1994), 13 and 140. Against Hayek's stated anti-Benthamism, Allison Dube argues their close proximity in Dube, *The Theme of Acquisitiveness in Bentham's Political Thought* (New York: Garland, 1991), 198–313.

14 Emma Rothschild, *Economic Sentiments: Adam Smith, Condorcet, and the Enlightenment* (Cambridge, MA: Harvard University Press, 2001), 65, quoting Beatrice (Potter) Webb, "The History of English Economics."

15 The break is broadly accepted outside the economics discipline, and from a range of perspectives. In addition to Webb and Rothschild see different treatments of Smith and after in Karl Polanyi, *The Great Transformation: The Political and Economic Origins of Our Time* (Boston: Beacon Press, 1944); Keith Tribe, *Land, Labour, and Economic Discourse* (Milton Park, Abingdon: Routledge & Kegan Paul, 1978); Elizabeth Anderson, *Private Government: How Employers Rule our Lives (and Why We Don't Talk about it)* (Princeton: Princeton University Press, 2017); Ute Tellman, *Life and Money: The Genealogy of the Liberal Economy and the Displacement of Politics* (New York: Columbia University Press, 2018).

16 See Stephen G. Engelmann, "Queer Utilitarianism: Bentham and Malthus on the Threshold of Biopolitics," *Theory and Event* 17:4 (2014).

17 Thus my concerns are very different from the back and forth re "analytic egalitarianism" in Sandra Peart and David Levy's stirring *The "Vanity of the Philosopher"* (Ann Arbor: Michigan University Press, 2005), as they are from most economists' celebrations of Smith.

18 Bentham, *Writings on Political Economy, Volume I*, 47.

19 On Smith, the exchange market, and the public realm see

Hannah Arendt, *The Human Condition*, 2nd edn. (Chicago: Chicago University Press, 1998), 160; on Smith and Aristotle's *Politics* see Samuel Fleischacker, *On Adam Smith's Wealth of Nations* (Princeton: Princeton University Press, 2004), 93.

20 Perhaps no one has given greater emphasis to this aspect of Smith's work and its importance for how to think about economic life than Deirdre McCloskey; see e.g. McCloskey's "Bourgeois Era" trilogy beginning with *The Bourgeois Virtues* (Chicago: University of Chicago Press, 2006–2016).

21 Aristotle, *The Politics of Aristotle,* ed. and trans. E. Barker (Oxford: Clarendon Press, 1946), 6.

22 Adam Smith, *Lectures on Jurisprudence*, R. L. Meek, D. D. Raphael, and P. G. Stein, eds. (Indianapolis: Liberty Fund reprint, 1982), (B) 56, 352. Hereafter referred to in text as "*LJ.*"

23 Karl Marx, *Capital, Volume I,* trans. B. Fowkes (London: Penguin Books, 1976), 280.

24 Jean Dunbabin, "The Reception and Interpretation of Aristotle's *Politics*," *The Cambridge History of Later Medieval Philosophy: From the Rediscovery of Aristotle to the Disintegration of Scholasticism, 1100–1600*, N. Kretzmann, A. Kenny, J. Pinborg, and E. Stump, eds. (Cambridge: Cambridge University Press, 1982), 721–737. Cicero's *De Officiis* was widely copied before the printing press, and following its invention it was the most printed book after the Bible.

25 The strictures of Aristotle and Xenophon regarding "political economy" were recognized and swept aside near the beginning of the first book to include the phrase in its title, Montchrestien's *Traicté de l'Économie Politique*; Stephen G. Engelmann, *Imagining Interest in Political Thought: Origins of Economic Rationality* (Durham: Duke University Press, 2003), 111.

26 In Smith's own lexicon, it should be said, "management," though hierarchical, is positively associated with persuasion and opposed to "force and violence" (*WN* V.i.g., 799).

27 Compare Aristotle, "He who is without a polis, by reason of his own nature ... at once plunges into a passion for war," *Politics*, 5.

28 "Bargain," in *Oxford English Dictionary*. 2nd edn., 20 vols. (Oxford: Oxford University Press, 1989), continually updated at http://www.oed.com/.

29 See the discussion of the contemporary *doux commerce* thesis in Albert O. Hirschman, *Passions and the Interests: Political Arguments for Capitalism Before its Triumph* (Princeton: Princeton University Press, 1977), 56–66.

30 This economic approach very consequentially made its way into US jurisprudence on antitrust, through courts' adoption of the "consumer welfare" standard from Robert Bork's *The Antitrust Paradox* (New York: Free Press, 1978). It is lately being challenged in Congress and the executive branch, restoring older concerns about market concentration and market power.

31 On this combination see Barbara Arneil, "Jeremy Bentham: Pauperism, Colonialism, and Imperialism," *American Political Science Review* 115:4 (2021), 1147–1158.

32 Lecturing on crime Smith attributes the frequency of murders in the Paris of his time to turned out servants, who are "the most helpless set of men imaginable," they are "depraved both in body and mind" by servility (*LJ* A.vi.5, 333). "Nothing tends so much to corrupt mankind as dependencey, while independencey still increases the honesty of the people. The establishment of commerce and manufactures, which brings about this independencey, is the best police for preventing crimes" (*LJ* B.204–205, 486–487).

33 Ian MacLean, *Adam Smith, Radical and Egalitarian: An Interpretation for the 21ˢᵗ Century* (London: Palgrave Macmillan, 2006), 27–45.

34 Smith, Bentham, and the whole tradition of political economy follow David Hume's critique of the original contract and its natural rights as fiction, for Bentham a dangerous fiction, "nonsense upon stilts." In this radical as opposed to revolutionary tradition, "(g)overnment's limit of competence will be bounded by the utility of governmental intervention [as opposed to whether it has a right to intervene] ... (T)he problem of English radicalism is the problem of utility." Michel Foucault, *The Birth of Biopolitics: Lectures at the Collège de France 1978–1979*, trans. G. Burchell (London: Palgrave Macmillan, 2008), 40.

35 Samuel Fleischacker, *Being Me Being You: Adam Smith and Empathy* (Chicago: University of Chicago Press, 2019).

36 Andreas Kalyvas and Ira Katznelson, *Liberal Beginnings: Making a Republic for the Moderns* (Cambridge: Cambridge University Press, 2008); Eric MacGilvray, *The Invention of Market Freedom* (Cambridge: Cambridge University Press, 2011).

37 Emma Rothschild, *Economic Sentiments: Adam Smith, Condorcet, and the Enlightenment*, 61–73.

38 See Dugald Stewart's insistence on this separation in Adam Smith, *The Theory of Moral Sentiments*, new edn., ed. D. Stewart (London: Henry G. Bohn, 1853), l–lxi.

39 William Godwin, *An Enquiry Concerning Political Justice*,

and Its Influence on General Virtue and Happiness, 2 vols. (London: G. G. J. and J. Robinson, 1793).

40 William Hazlitt, *A Reply to the Essay on Population, by the Rev. T. R. Malthus* (London: Longman, 1807), 61.

41 William Godwin, *Thoughts Occasioned by the Perusal of Dr. Parr's Spital Sermon* ... (London: Taylor and Wilks, 1801).

42 Anthony Waterman, *Revolution, Economics and Religion: Christian Political Economy, 1798–1833* (Cambridge: Cambridge University Press, 1991).

43 T. R. Malthus, *An Essay on the Principle of Population ...,* new edn., very much enlarged (London: J. Johnson, 1803).

44 Jane Haldimand Marcet, *Conversations on Political Economy; in Which the Elements of that Science are Familiarly Explained,* 6th edn. (London: Longman, 1827), hereafter *CPE* in text; Jean-Baptiste Say, *A Treatise on Political Economy,* 4th edn., trans. C. R. Prinsep (Philadelphia: Lippincott, Gramo & Co., 1855), xlvin.

45 See also Jane Haldimand Marcet, *John Hopkins's Notions on Political Economy* (London: Longman, 1833).

46 Say, *A Treatise on Political Economy,* xv.

47 Richard Whatmore, *Republicanism and the French Revolution: An Intellectual History of Jean-Baptiste Say's Political Economy* (Oxford: Oxford University Press, 2000), 214.

48 David Ricardo, *An Essay on The Influence of a low Price of Corn on the Profits of Stock,* 2nd edn. (London: John Murray, 1815), 20 and 49–50.

49 David Ricardo, *On the Principles of Political Economy and Taxation* (London: John Murray, 1817), 112–113.

50 Nassau Senior, *Political Economy,* 3rd edn. (London and Glasgow: Richard Griffin, 1851), 59.

51 And note that a fellow radical like John Thelwall of the London Corresponding Society could already in his 1796 publication, *The Rights of Nature,* bridge Lockean natural rights with a Smithian embrace of economic modernization to develop proto-Marxian arguments, asserting that "'the hideous accumulation of capital in a few hands ... carries, in its own enormity, the seeds of cure'" in the increasing mutual education and politicization of laborers. John Thelwall, *The Rights of Nature,* quoted in Iain Hampsher-Monk, "John Thewall and the Eighteenth-Century Radical Response to Political Economy," *The Historical Journal* 34:1 (1991), 18.

52 Francis Place, *Illustrations and Proofs of the Principle of Population* (London: Longman, 1822), 8, 169–172, and passim.

53 John Stuart Mill, *Newspaper Writings, December 1822–July 1831* (*The Collected Works of John Stuart Mill* [hereafter CW], vol. XXII), A. P. Robson and J. M. Robson, eds. (Toronto: University of Toronto Press, 1986), 80–91.

54 John Stuart Mill, *Principles of Political Economy with Some of Their Applications to Social Philosophy* (*CW*, vols. II and III), ed. J. M. Robson (Toronto: University of Toronto Press, 1965); hereafter *PPE* in notes and text.

55 John Stuart Mill, *Essays on Economics and Society* (*CW*, vol. IV), ed. J. M. Robson (Toronto: University of Toronto Press, 1967), 326; hereafter *DPE* in text.

56 Charles Devas, *Groundwork of Economics* (Harlow: Longmans, 1883), 26–27; "Homo economicus," in *Oxford English Dictionary*. It's ironic that Devas calls Mill's figure the "dollar-hunting animal," when this recalls none other than Mill himself, disparaging pre-Civil War American men (*PPE* 754n).

57 This is the lesson of the "art of measurement" from Plato's *Protagoras*, admired (and translated) by the younger Mill and referenced at the outset of his 1861 essay on utilitarianism; John Stuart Mill, *Essays on Philosophy and the Classics* (*CW*, vol. XI), ed. J. M. Robson (Toronto: University of Toronto Press, 1978), 39–61; John Stuart Mill, *Essays on Ethics, Religion and Society* (*CW*, vol. X), ed. J. M. Robson (Toronto: University of Toronto Press, 1985), 205.

58 David Ricardo, *On the Principles of Political Economy, and Taxation*, 3rd edn. (London: John Murray, 1821), 466–482. Ricardo does conclude the discussion with reasons why this should not "lead to the inference that machinery should not be encouraged" (478).

59 John Stuart Mill, *Essays on Politics and Society Part I* (*CW*, vol. XVIII), ed. J. M. Robson (Toronto: University of Toronto Press, 1977), 224.

60 John Stuart Mill, *Essays on Economics and Society Part II* (*CW*, vol. VI), ed. J. M. Robson (Toronto: University of Toronto Press, 1967), 703–753; see generally Joseph Persky, *The Political Economy of Progress: John Stuart Mill and Modern Radicalism* (Oxford: Oxford University Press, 2016).

61 William Thompson, *Appeal of One Half of the Human Race, Women, Against the Pretentions of the Other Half, Men ...* (London: Longman, 1825).

62 Hirschman, *The Passions and the Interests*; for a more directly political account of early-modern interest that builds on yet

departs from Hirschman's, see Engelmann, *Imagining Interest in Political Thought.*

63 John Stuart Mill, *A System of Logic Part II* (CW, vol. VIII), ed. J. M. Robson (Toronto: University of Toronto Press, 1974), 889–890.

64 See e.g. John Stuart Mill, *Essays on Ethics, Religion and Society* (CW, vol. X), ed. J. M. Robson (Toronto: University of Toronto Press, 1985), 112–113.

65 These show up first in civil law writings, then in the political economy, and finally are recognized as general subordinate ends for the entire Pannomion, or complete code of laws. See e.g. their presence in the (mostly) late manuscripts that were published by posthumous editors as "Pannomial Fragments"; *Selected Writings: Jeremy Bentham*, ed. S. G. Engelmann (New Haven: Yale University Press, 2011), 240–280.

66 Jeremy Bentham, *Rationale of Judicial Evidence*. In *The Works of Jeremy Bentham, Volume VII*, ed. J. Bowring (Edinburgh: William Tait, 1838–1843), 334.

67 Jeremy Bentham, "Offences Against One's Self," ed. L. Crompton, *Journal of Homosexuality* 3 (1978), 389–406 and 4 (1978), 91–107; see also Bentham, *Of Sexual Irregularities, and Other Writings on Sexual Morality* (CW), P. Schofield, C. Pease-Watkin, and M. Quinn, eds. (Oxford: Oxford University Press, 2014) and Bentham, *Not Paul, But Jesus*, vol. III (London: Bentham Project, UCL, 2013), https://discovery.ucl.ac.uk/id/eprint/1392179/3/npbj.pdf.

68 Jeremy Bentham, *Writings on Political Economy, Volume I*, 53.

69 Jeremy Bentham, *An Introduction to the Principles of Morals and Legislation* (CW), J. H. Burns and H. L. A. Hart, eds. (Oxford: Clarendon Press, 1996), 173–174.

70 Steven E. Landsburg, *The Armchair Economist*, quoted in Mankiw, *Principles of Economics*, 5.

71 Jon Elster, "Leibniz and the Development of Economic Rationality," *Trends in Western Civilization Program*, no. 5 (Oslo: University of Oslo, 1975), 5–9.

72 Jeremy Bentham, *Official Aptitude Maximized; Expense Minimized* (CW), ed. P. Schofield (Oxford: Oxford University Press, 1993).

73 Adam Smith, *LJ* A.i.3–4, 6.

74 Jeremy Bentham, *The Collected Works of Jeremy Bentham: Rights, Representation, and Reform: Nonsense Upon Stilts and Other Writings on the French Revolution*, P. Schofield,

C. Pease-Watkin, and C. Blamires, eds. (Oxford: Oxford University Press, 2002), 317–401.

75 Jeremy Bentham, "Indirect Legislation," c. 1782, University College London Bentham Collection, see e.g. Box 87, folio 169: "Publication of the prices of commodities. Against Extortion in the way of trade."

76 Jane K. Elliott, *The Microeconomic Mode Political Subjectivity in Contemporary Popular Aesthetics* (New York: Columbia University Press, 2018), 10.

4 Economics as Politics

1 Already in 1800 the French diplomat Alexandre d'Hauterive could see political economy as an "adjunct of English power, a pretext for 'interfering in the most important relations of the social, administrative and political organization of all nations,'" Emma Rothschild, "Political Economy," in Gareth Stedman Jones and Gregory Claeys, eds., *The Cambridge History of Nineteenth-Century Political Thought* (Cambridge: Cambridge University Press, 2011), 752. German economist Friedrich List was a noted skeptic of commercial cosmopolitanism and very influential during his American exile in legitimating the protectionist and other strategies that, on most historical accounts, were crucial to US industrial development. In addition, throughout the nineteenth century, popular challenges and appropriations in England and abroad questioned political economy's class basis and blind spots. Elements of plural approaches found their way into the British mainstream through John Stuart Mill's and Alfred Marshall's canonical syntheses.

2 Lorraine Daston and Peter Gallison, *Objectivity* (New York: Zone Books, 2007).

3 Sophia Mihic, Stephen G. Engelmann, and Elizabeth Rose Wingrove, "Facts, Values, and 'Real' Numbers: Making Sense in and of Political Science," in *The Politics of Method in the Human Sciences: Positivism and its Epistemological Others*, ed. George Steinmetz (Durham: Duke University Press, 2005), 470–496.

4 There is a huge literature here, but see with special relevance to economics Hilary Putnam, *The Collapse of the Fact/Value Dichotomy and Other Essays* (Cambridge, MA: Harvard University Press, 2002). New attacks on the fact/value dichotomy arose in political science in the 1960s and 1970s; for two classic statements see William E. Connolly, *The Terms of*

Political Discourse, revd. edn. (Princeton: Princeton University Press, 1993) and Charles Taylor, "Neutrality in Political Science," in *Philosophical Papers: Volume 2, Philosophy and the Human Sciences* (Cambridge: Cambridge University Press, 1985), 58–90. The response of the mainstream has been largely to misunderstand, contain, or ignore such attacks; see Mihic et al., "Facts, Values, and 'Real' Numbers."

5 On Robbins' life and career see Susan Howson, *Lionel Robbins* (Cambridge: Cambridge University Press, 2011).

6 Lionel Robbins, *An Essay on the Nature and Significance of Economic Science*, 3rd edn. (New York: New York University Press, 1984), 16 (hereafter *NS* in text). On the bumpy route to widespread acceptance by the 1960s of what was in its time a highly controversial argument see Roger E. Backhouse and Steve G. Medema, "Defining Economics: The Long Road to Acceptance of the Robbins Definition," *Economica* 76 (2009), 805–820.

7 Howson, *Lionel Robbins*, 166–206; Frank H. Knight, "The Theory of Choice and Exchange," in *Risk, Uncertainty and Profit* (Boston: Hart, Schaffner & Marx, 1921), 51–94.

8 Frank H. Knight, review of *The Nature and Significance of Economic Science* by Lionel Robbins, *International Journal of Ethics* 44:3 (1934), 358–361. There is no reason to think that Knight was moved by any revisions to the second edition, see brief review of *The Nature and Significance of Economic Science* by Lionel Robbins, *American Journal of Sociology* 42:3 (1936), 425.

9 Knight in an aside to a remarkable review essay on economic positivism distinguishes, as really no one else in the literature seems to do, between the instrumentality of technical rationality and this peculiar trait of economic rationality; Frank H. Knight, "What is 'Truth' in Economics?," *Journal of Political Economy* 48:1 (1940), 16n. See also Knight, "The Nature of Economic Science in Some Recent Discussion," *American Economic Review* 24:2 (1934), 228–229. The confusion noted by Knight between what people generally understand to be ends or objectives and the "end" of economizing is still present in Gregory Mankiw's much-used textbook. Mankiw introduces the rationality assumption by defining "rational people," who "think at the margin" as "people who systematically and purposefully do the best they can to achieve their objectives," N. Gregory Mankiw, *Principles of Economics*, 9th edn. (Boston: Cengage Learning, 2021), 4.

10 I argue that all economists, including Austrians, who work in the postclassical "choice" tradition adhere more or less rigorously to the subjective theory of value; Knight is unusual for his clarity of understanding of this allocative framing as itself a political endeavor. For a particularly clear and rigorous non-Austrian statement of the implications of the subjective theory of value for the discipline, unbothered by Knight's fact/value queries, see James M. Buchanan, *Cost and Choice: An Inquiry in Economic Theory* (Chicago: University of Chicago Press, 1969).

For a classic Austrian statement of the failures, and their consequences, of any attempt to make trade-offs for others see Friedrich Hayek, "The Use of Knowledge in Society," *American Economic Review* 35:4 (1945), 519–530.

11 Rational action, as the Austrian purist Ludwig von Mises understands it, is a "pleonasm"; nothing really could count as evidence against it. It is simply and self-evidently true for Mises that action is moved by "unease"; compare John Locke, as read by Uday Singh Mehta in *The Anxiety of Freedom* (Ithaca, NY: Cornell University Press, 1992). The actor looks for satisfaction, the relief of unease, in choosing what is most valued among alternatives by them at any one time and in any one place. Mises' "praxeology" explicitly covers all of human conduct, which it construes in terms of moving through a world that always demands and elicits allocative choice; the text is thus very much in Jane Elliott's "microeconomic mode" (Elliott, *The Microeconomic Mode: Political Subjectivity in Contemporary Popular Aesthetics* [New York: Columbia University Press, 2018)]. That said, Mises is rigorously opposed to any suggestion of an implied psychology or an implied hierarchy of value (which would in any case be unique to the individual), and to any imputation of operational metrics: choice is according to preferences that are only comparatively – with regard to the choices presented – and not absolutely, ranked. Anything that most satisfies the ordinal valuation of that individual in that moment, whether martyr or miser, is, however, what they do. See von Mises, *Human Action: A Treatise on Economics* (New Haven: Yale University Press, 1949).

12 Choice and commensurability are present across basic contemporary economic teaching, despite a variety of approaches to rationality; see, for example, the range of perspectives detailed in Martin K. Jones, "The Concept of Rationality in Introductory Economics Textbooks," *Citizenship, Social and Economics Education* 20:1 (2021), 37–47.

13 Knight, "The Nature of Economic Science in Some Recent Discussion," 236.

14 Timothy Mitchell, "The Properties of Markets," *Do Economists Make Markets?: On the Performativity of Economics,* D. MacKenzie, F. Muniesa, and L. Siu, eds. (Princeton: Princeton University Press, 2007), 244.

15 The economist will point out that in the face of a call to duty one might not be able to exit, but one can (and so presumably will, without attached penalty?) minimize costs and shirk by "free-riding" on the masks and vaccines of others if enough are used. See Mancur Olson, *The Logic of Collective Action: Public Goods and the Theory of Groups* (Cambridge, MA: Harvard University Press, 1965). Olson's text has inspired a huge volume of research in political science, and even entered everyday discourse. For a critique that shows in various respects how peculiar – even in the history of rationalist individualism – the assumptions are that drive this postwar artifact and their connection to disciplinary mutations in economics (in particular, the rise of the idea of perfect competition), see Richard Tuck, *Free Riding* (Cambridge, MA: Harvard University Press, 2008).

16 William D. Nordhaus, "Climate change: the Ultimate Challenge for Economics," Prize Lecture (2018). https://www.nobelprize.org/uploads/2018/10/nordhaus-lecture.pdf.

17 New work in historical sociology is amassing evidence for this point; see Stephanie L. Mudge, *Leftism Reinvented: Leftist Parties from Socialism to Neoliberalism* (Cambridge, MA: Harvard University Press, 2018) and Elizabeth Popp Berman, *Thinking like an Economist: How Efficiency Replaced Equality in U.S. Public Policy* (Princeton: Princeton University Press, 2022).

18 For example, *Thinking like an Economist* flags the importance of the emergence and proliferation of university public policy and policy studies programs, which center mainstream economic literacy in their training, 62–66.

19 Susan Howson, "The Origins of Lionel Robbins's *Essay on the Nature and Significance of Economic Science*," *History of Political Economy* 36:3 (2004), 413–443.

20 For needed caution on any assimilation of the three theorists to one another see William Jaffe, "Menger, Jevons and Walras De-Homogenized," *Economic Inquiry* 14 (1976), 511–524.

21 From his earliest work forward Nobelist Amartya Sen, Indian economist and philosopher, has criticized mainstream economics for its foundations and methods and their continuing connection

to stunted conceptions of welfare. He has made numerous contributions, including the development of a distinctive, somewhat Millian, "capabilities" approach, which emphasizes a common interest in building capacities for flourishing for all people.

22 The Kingdom of Bhutan, for example, measures Gross National Happiness.

23 "Art and science" is very much Bentham's (and J. S. Mill's) contemporary phraseology; "conduct of conduct" I borrow, as a definition of government broadly understood, from Michel Foucault, *Government of the Living: Lectures at the Collège de France 1979–1980*, ed. Michel Senellart, trans. Graham Burchell (Basingstoke: Palgrave Macmillan, 2014), 12.

24 On causation and practical science see R. G. Collingwood, *An Essay on Metaphysics* (Oxford, Oxford University Press, 1940).

25 See John Stuart Mill, *A System of Logic, Ratiocinative and Inductive*, ed. John Robson, *Collected Works of John Stuart Mill*, vol. VIII (Toronto: University of Toronto Press, 1974), 944.

26 John Bowring, ed., *Deontology; or the Science of Morality... From the Mss. of Jeremy Bentham*, 2 vols. (Edinburgh: William Tait, 1834). The idea that Bentham is a "normative" moral philosopher in the modern sense comes from a history of reading, appropriation, and elaboration of a minute percentage of his work, that is, a few early chapters of Bentham, *An Introduction to the Principles of Morals and Legislation*, eds. J. H. Burns and H. L. A. Hart (London: The Athlone Press, 1970), *Collected Works of Jeremy Bentham* (hereafter *CW*).

27 Jeremy Bentham, *An Introduction to the Principles of Morals and Legislation*, 215n.

28 This is the utilitarian theory of crime that descends from Cesare Beccaria and reappears in Chicago economist Gary Becker's work. Becker notoriously argues for and accepts an efficient amount of crime; Bentham is no utopian but he doesn't think in terms of efficient crime, because perhaps the most serious consequence of crime is the secondary "alarm" effect on public security. At one level, Becker's view is consonant with Bentham's thinking: alarm is for Bentham in principle measurable, and Becker would presumably think he could measure it. But Bentham might be alarmed that security qua security is not even a consideration in Becker's radically economic starting point, which doesn't think of crime as a security-upsetting violation, exactly, just a cost (in burglary's

case of the zero-sum transactions plus investments in locks plus investments in picking locks, etc.). Compare Bentham, *An Introduction to the Principles of Morals and Legislation*, 143–157, and the following from Becker: "In the early stages of my work on crime, I was puzzled by why theft is socially harmful since it appears merely to redistribute resources ... I resolved the puzzle ... by recognizing that criminals spend ... and that such spending is unproductive." Gary S. Becker, "Nobel Lecture: The Economic Way of Looking at Behavior," *Journal of Political Economy* 101:3 (1993), 391.

29 I borrow the language of disenchantment from William Davies' *The Limits of Neoliberalism* (London: Sage Publications, 2014). As Stephanie Mudge notes, the distinctive Davies approach to neoliberalism understands it as a "project to undermine value-rational notions of the common good via economic theories, argumentation, and calculation, remaking all action as economic action regardless of context." Thus on this political-sociological reading, "neoliberalism" goes well beyond the work of economists of the Right. "Roundtable: The Limits of Neo-Liberalism," *Renewal: A Journal of Social Democracy* 22:3/4 (2014), 88.

30 One of the consequences of economic disenchantment is to "imbue liberal political institutions with an inherently limited form of political legitimacy that ... can justify just about anything except those institutions' own existence." Mudge, "Roundtable: The Limits of Neo-Liberalism," 88.

31 Compare Anthony Simon Laden, *Reasoning: A Social Picture* (Oxford: Oxford University Press, 2012).

32 Frank Knight, already seeing this specter early on, reads entre-preneurial activity as exceptional in its genuine uncertainty, and thus uniquely value-adding; it is the exception then that proves the rule for and of the rest of us. See Knight, *Risk, Uncertainty and Profit*.

33 Frank H. Knight, 1934 review of Robbins, 360–361.

34 Lionel Robbins, "Economics and Political Economy," Richard T. Ely lecture delivered to the American Economic Association first published in *American Economic Review* (1981), reprinted in Robbins, *Nature and Significance of Economic Science*, 3rd edn., xi–xxxiii.

35 See Lionel Robbins, "Introduction," in Philip H. Wicksteed, *The Common Sense of Political Economy and Selected Papers and Reviews on Economic Theory*, vol. I, ed. L. Robbins (New York: Augustus M. Kelly reprint, 1967 [1933]). Robbins says of the

title, "never was a work of this kind more unfortunately named. It is not 'common sense' in the ordinary sense of the term, and it is not *political* economy" (xi–xii) (emphasis in original).

36 LSE was also famously in opposition to strains of work active at the powerful Cambridge department (the circle around J. M. Keynes); the differences grew sharper as crisis put new pressure on debates and on economic theory itself.

37 Philip H. Wicksteed, "Das Kapital: A Criticism," *To-Day* 2:10 (1884), 388–411. This preceded Eugen von Böhm-Bawerk's more well-known critique of Marx and was, according to Robbins, Wicksteed's first contribution to economic theory.

38 See the Jevons and Wicksteed entries on Gonçalo L. Fonseca's History of Economic Thought website, http://www.hetwebsite. net/het/.

39 "The untutored savage, like the child, is wholly occupied with the pleasures and the troubles of the moment; the morrow is dimly felt ...," W. Stanley Jevons, *The Theory of Political Economy*, 5th edn. (New York: Augustus M. Kelley reprint, 1965 [1871, 1879]), 35 (hereafter referred to in text as *TPE*).

40 Moral and physical are the categories in J. S. Mill's monumental *Logic*, which went through eight editions from 1843 through 1872. They don't neatly map our "social" versus "natural" sciences.

41 Philip Mirowski, *More Heat than Light: Economics as Social Physics, Physics as Nature's Economics* (Cambridge: Cambridge University Press, 1989).

42 In the 1879 preface he credits Continental economics as being way ahead in this regard (for example his correspondent Walras, and before him Augustin Cournot).

43 The vast literature bringing formal methods to thinking about institutions, straddling economics and political science, generally goes by the name "neo-institutionalism." But at least in political science, agent-based modelling is not completely a matter of allocative choosing. Even the de-institutionalized re-institutionalizing game theory of Robert Axelrod's *Evolution of Cooperation* (New York: Basic Books, 1984) models agents as quasi-strategic rather than strictly economic actors. If we take the metaphor of a game seriously, and especially if the game is a competitive game and we are playing to win, then that singular end violates the rule of commensurability: it can't be traded off under any circumstances (other ends are simply subsumed to winning, and trade-offs are only between things that are useful to winning). Thus some wings of the

literature are decidedly more political in their orientation, to continue the metaphor, to a common field of play, than others. However, even more political game theory might well make the sometimes incorrect assumption that all players are playing the same game, which can contribute to poor analysis and strategic disaster. If "rational-choice" political science in the US owed its rise to the early Cold War (Sonjae Amadae, *Rationalizing Capitalist Democracy* [Chicago: University of Chicago Press, 2003]), perhaps reverberations from US imperial losses have contributed to its dethroning.

44 Jevons references these texts as foundational for his thinking, but without highlighting the direct links to his own work that I specify here.

45 Jeremy Bentham, *Codification Proposal, Addressed by Jeremy Bentham to All Nations Professing Liberal Opinions* (London: J. M'Creery, 1822), 9–10.

46 Jeremy Bentham, *A Table of the Springs of Action* (London: R. Hunter, 1817), 5 (emphasis in original).

47 Thomas Dixon, *The Invention of Altruism: Making Moral Meanings in Victorian Britain* (Oxford: Oxford University Press, 2008).

48 In the Table itself fourteen pleasures/pains and their corresponding interests, some quite social (e.g. amity, sympathy, antipathy) or spiritual (e.g. curiosity, piety), are analytically distinguished even as they are, for the agent, commensurable components of a single motivating interest or "balance on the side of good."

49 "(I)t is no otherwise than through the medium of the *imagination*, that any pleasure, or any pain, is capable of operating in the character of a *motive*," *A Table of the Springs of Action*, 4 (emphasis in original). Thus the basis for Jevons' "estimation" of what "promises" greater pleasure, and how for economics generally, the future isn't even future. Bentham's contemporary (and sometime tenant) William Hazlitt takes reliance upon the imagination to its logical conclusion in a virtuoso deconstruction of the self of self-interest; see Hazlitt, *An Essay on the Principles of Human Action* (London: J. Johnson, 1805), 32.

50 Bentham manuscript quoted in Robbins' 1981 lecture (*NS*, xxii); see also Lionel Robbins, *The Evolution of Modern Economic Theory* (London: Macmillan & Co., 1970), 81.

51 Philip Henry Wicksteed, *The Common Sense of Political Economy, Including a Study of the Human Basis of Economic Law* (London: Macmillan & Co., 1910), 32.

52 Benjamin Franklin, "From Benjamin Franklin to Joseph Priestly, 19 September 1772," National Archives (website), https://founders.archives.gov/documents/Franklin/01-19-02-0200.

53 That is, the Menger/Wieser/Von Mises tradition rests on the idea of intra-subjective commensurability, which is a basic assumption of all subjective value theory.

54 See especially Gary S. Becker, "A Theory of the Allocation of Time," *Economic Journal* 75:299 (1965), 493–517; *The Economic Approach to Human Behavior* (Chicago: University of Chicago Press, 1976); "Nobel Lecture: The Economic Way of Looking at Behavior."

55 John D. Mueller, *Redeeming Economics: Rediscovering the Missing Element* (New York: Open Road Media, 2014).

56 Wicksteed, *The Common Sense of Political Economy*, 409.

57 Martha C. Nussbaum, "The Costs of Tragedy: Some Moral Limits of Cost-Benefit Analysis," *Journal of Legal Studies* 29:S2 (2000), 1005–1036.

58 Putnam, *The Collapse of the Fact/Value Dichotomy*, 53 (emphasis in original).

59 Ibid., 54 (emphasis in original).

60 This was the subject of an early debate between George Stigler and Paul Samuelson (Stigler thought the new welfare economics should be called "applied ethics"); Eric Schliesser, "The Separation of Economics from Virtue: A Historical–Conceptual Introduction" in Jennifer A. Baker and Mark D. White, eds., *Economics and the Virtues: Building a New Moral Foundation* (Oxford: Oxford University Press, 2016), 152–154.

61 Robbins, Ely lecture, *NS* xxii–iii.

62 The problem is a long-recognized one, and already at the time of the Robbins lecture colleagues were bringing envy into their calculations; see, for example, Hal Ronald Varian, "Equity, Envy, and Efficiency," *Journal of Economic Theory* 9:1 (1974), 63–91.

63 Robbins, Ely lecture, *NS* xxiii.

64 A monumental early exemplar of this approach is Kenneth J. Arrow's "A Difficulty in the Concept of Social Welfare," *Journal of Political Economy* 58:4 (1950), 328–346. For a dazzling and thoroughly researched account of the political and technological origins and consequences of developments in postwar economics see Philip Mirowski, *Machine Dreams: Economics Becomes a Cyborg Science* (Cambridge: Cambridge University Press, 2002).

65 On revealed preference see D. Wade Hands, "Paul Samuelson

and Revealed Preference Theory," *History of Political Economy* 46:1, 85–116. Hands delves into the mystery of Samuelson's apparent retreat from what originally looked like a root-and-branch attack on utility theory in economics. In any case the range of debate, and the varied contemporary interpretations of what revealed preference is and implies, all reinforce choice as the fulcrum for any consideration of rationality.

66 See e.g. James M. Buchanan and Gordon Tullock, *The Calculus of Consent: Logical Foundations of Constitutional Democracy* (Ann Arbor: University of Michigan Press, 1962).

67 Davies, *The Limits of Neoliberalism*, 4. See Tuck, *Free Riding* for an account of how twentieth-century economics transformed what had been for its political-economic and utilitarian predecessors a comfort with the individual rationality of collective action.

68 *Hume's Treatise of Human Nature*, ed. L. A. Selby-Bigge (London: Henry Frowde, 1896 [1739]), 415–416 (II.iii.3). That this preference for my lesser good is not, needless to say, necessarily stable renders it unassimilable even to the barest "consistency" account of economic rationality.

69 Alan Kirman, *Complex Economics: Individual and Collective Rationality* (Milton Park, Abingdon: Routledge, 2010), 12.

70 Plato, *Protagoras and Meno*, trans. Adam Beresford (New York: Penguin, 2006), 18.

71 Well aware of the history and etymology of "economy," Friedrich Hayek refused the label in favor of "catallaxy"; see, for example, Hayek, *Studies in Philosophy, Politics and Economics* (Chicago: University of Chicago Press, 1967), 164. But any consideration of Hayek's long career, for example his correspondence with Margaret Thatcher after her ascendancy to the prime minister's office in the UK in 1979, betrays his readiness to offer expert advice in political-economic management (see letters from Hayek to Thatcher dated 28 August 1979 and 24 April 1980 on trade union and monetary policy, https://www.margaretthatcher.org).

72 "About Cato," Cato Institute (website), https://www.cato.org/about.

73 The contradiction is always present, but comes out most clearly in times of crisis. See, for example, Dieter Plehwe's report and analysis in "Neoliberal Think Tanks and the Crisis," in Roger E. Backhouse, Bradley W. Bateman, Tamotsu Nishizawa, and Dieter Plehwe, eds., *Liberalism and the Welfare State:*

Economists and Arguments for the Welfare State (Oxford: Oxford University Press, 2017), 191–211.

74 James Madison, "Federalist Papers No. 10," Bill of Rights Institute (website), https://billofrightsinstitute.org/primary-sources/federalist-no-10.

75 Frank Knight, review of Robbins, 359.

76 See also Lionel Robbins, *The Economic Basis of Class Conflict and other Essays in Political Economy* (London: Macmillan & Co., 1939), v–28.

77 See Daniel Kahneman, *Thinking, Fast and Slow* (New York: Farrar, Straus and Giroux, 2011). The behavioral economist Richard Thaler acknowledges his debt to the psychologists Kahneman and longtime collaborator Amos Tversky throughout Thaler, *Misbehaving: The Making of Behavioral Economics* (New York: W. W. Norton, 2015).

5 Conclusion

1 Gary S. Becker, *The Economic Approach to Human Behavior* (Chicago: University of Chicago Press, 1976), 9–10 (emphasis in original). Remember, the committed worker might be working in service to others; the passage assumes neither selfishness nor selflessness in the usual senses.

2 Samuel A. Chambers, "Undoing Neoliberalism: *Homo Œconomicus, Homo Politicus, and the Zōon Politikon,*" *Critical Inquiry* 44:4 (2018), 706–732.

3 See the forcefully republican political reading of fetishism-as-domination given by William Clare Roberts in *Marx's Inferno: The Political Theory of* Capital (Princeton: Princeton University Press, 2017), 85–93.

4 Chambers, "Undoing Neoliberalism," 731–732; Anand Giridharadas, *Winners Take All: The Elite Charade of Changing the World* (New York: Knopf, 2018).

5 Milton Friedman, *Capitalism and Freedom* (Chicago: University of Chicago Press, 1962), 2.

6 This holds true in principle for any number of trivial to non-trivial "public" effects from "private" exchange practices: technical, pecuniary, positive, negative, etc.

7 See Quinn Slobodian, *Globalists: The End of Empire and the Birth of Neoliberalism* (Cambridge, MA: Harvard University Press, 2018); consider also the disturbing political implications of the first chapter alone of Adam Tooze, *Crashed: How*

a Decade of Financial Crises Changed the World (New York: Viking, 2018), 1–22.

8 Yuval Levin interview, National Public Radio, January 30, 2020 (transcript), https://www.npr.org/2020/01/30/800922222/when-institutions-are-used-as-stages-people-lose-trust-book-argues.

9 Keeanga-Yamahtta Taylor, participant, "Where Do We Go From Here: A Fundraiser for Black Lives," Harvard Book Store, https://www.youtube.com/watch?v=Er2jE4B9kDA (no transcript, at 121:30).

10 "'The evidence has piled up in such a way that it's maybe not unreasonable to call some of America's wealthiest people oligarchs. I think that's the way I'd put it ... *Lots* of evidence.'" Benjamin Page, quoted in Jaime Lowe, "With 'Stealth Politics,' Billionaires Make Sure Their Money Talks," *New York Times Magazine*, April 6, 2022, https://www.nytimes.com/2022/04/06/magazine/billionaire-politics.html. For a developed theory of oligarchy see Jeffrey A. Winters, *Oligarchy* (Cambridge: Cambridge University Press, 2011).

Index

Notes are indicated by the use of 'n.' after the page number, followed by the note number.